Southern Gothic
Stories from a Place Called Dixie

Elizabeth Carpenter Piechocinski

ISBN 978-1-9393060-4-3

Library of Congress Catalog Number: 2014935433

First Edition

Printed in the United States of America
Published by 23 House Publishing
SAN 299-8084
www.23house.com

Gothic:

The gothic novel, as a literary form, became popular in the 1800s and usually included elements of suspense, dark castles, ghostly dungeons, and damsels in distress who were rescued by handsome, brooding men haunted by some great tragedy in their lives. A good measure of romantic intrigue was also an essential part of the gothic novel. Novels such as these are as popular today as they were in the nineteenth century, although they have been adapted to the modern world. The gothic theme carried over into the art world with Grant Wood's well-known painting, *American Gothic.*

Southern Gothic, while not a novel, is quite at home in the gothic genre in that these tales include mystery, suspense, ghosts, murder, and an idealistic view of life as well. It differs however in the inclusion of a little tongue-in-cheek humor as well. In addition, these tales are based in fact.

Dedication

This book is dedicated to my mother who spent many hours telling us stories of her own childhood in a little country town in Georgia. Stories about her family members are much too poignant and revealing to omit. It was from her that I first began to listen to the tales of an era that was totally foreign to me, but very much alive in her own memories. It was there that my love of history was first nurtured.

This collection of tales and legends and history is also for my nephew Bill, his wife Crystal, and grandnephews William, Gregory and Benjamin, and my young grandniece, Savannah, who love to listen to old stories about their family and events of the past. Perhaps through these vignettes, they may come to know from whence they came. None of these stories is fictitious, although a few may border on the incredulous.

I also dedicate this collection to my husband John who kept encouraging me to complete this collection of lore that he felt should be set down so that it did not pass into obscurity. Some of these stories are his. Unfortunately, he did not live to see this book in print.

Finally, this book is dedicated to all of those kindly Southern souls who contributed, perhaps unwittingly, to being forever immortalized in this compilation of all things Southern. For the most part, these are all Southern stories. This book is from Dixie, with love.

– Sissy

.

Table of Contents

Foreword

This is a Southern book about the South. It is important that our oral history be recorded for posterity. This is not a conceit of only famous figures, but also the responsibility of ordinary people. It is essential to evaluating ourselves and to recording information that might be lost forever. After all, we seldom keep diaries as many of our ancestors did. Those who follow in our footsteps will never understand the previous generation if its mysteries, joys, sorrows, and legends are not recorded.

All of the stories contained herein are not totally reminiscences, but also include a compilation of obscure, human interest stories that otherwise might remain forever buried in some archives collection, to be read only when a scholar or researcher happens upon them in pursuit of other information. Some of these, I literally stumbled upon. Others were brought to my attention by those who knew of my lifelong interest in stories that are not so well known, but were worthy of attention. The book was designed that so a reader does not have to read the book cover to cover, but may read those sections that have greatest appeal for that individual. I would hope that one would read all of it, but I wanted it to be a book that people could open to any part and find something of interest. The tales recounted here are all true, although some may seem a bit improbable.

No harm was intended in my depictions of those very real characters who figure rather prominently in some of these tales. This is about real people, mostly Southerners. Their stories and

1

lives are important in this Southern chronicle, and no political statements are intended. This is our South and all of us have a stake in her future. The more we know of our fellow travelers on this planet, the greater is our connection to the human race. How important it is to know these people through their stories. It is a humbling situation when we observe that there are truly "no new things under the sun." Shakespeare got it right when he says that there were more things on earth than dreamed of in any philosophy.

Parts of this book are autobiographical, not that I believe my own life was so worthy of writing about, but because the stories fit the criteria of being in and of the South. They were probably typical of many young Southerners growing up in the first half of the twentieth century. Yes, some are humorous, some are a bit nostalgic, and perhaps too many people some of these may seem downright ridiculous. For younger readers some of the stories may seem like alien territory. But, if we can't poke fun at ourselves, and if we can't laugh at our own foibles, then perhaps we are taking our precious existence far too seriously and need to lighten up a bit.

So, find a comfortable chair, sit back, and be prepared for the stories that await you. Hopefully you will find them educational and entertaining, or if all else fails, they may be used to combat insomnia. Whatever your reaction may be, may you gain some insight into what makes at least some Southerners tick. When you discover the answer to this conundrum, please let me in on the secret. You will come to realize through all of this that we firmly believe that it is one of God's greatest blessings that He allowed us to be born Southern.

Introduction

People have always been fascinated with tales of the unusual, tales of those events that leave an impression on one's store of memories. Even though we live in a society where the internet, cell phones, and television dominate our daily lives, we still like to listen to a good story or to the reminiscences sparked by a chance remark or a faded newspaper clipping. Good conversation provides food for the imagination and leads the listener on a journey into bygone days when life was uncomplicated by a modern technology that only produces artificial entertainment. If this seems overly idyllic in terms of modern life, perhaps that is because it was an idyllic time in comparison with the way young people grow up today. Naiveté has its place, though it is now considered old-fashioned.

This book is an attempt to compile in a single volume the conversations and stories I heard in childhood, along with those I accumulated as an adult while researching materials for other books. With few exceptions, the experiences and stories I relate here have their roots firmly entrenched in our beloved Southern soil, and thus, reflect to a large degree, the people who lived these experiences. While this book is autobiographical to some extent, it is first and foremost the story of our Southern culture, our people, our legends, and our eccentricities. Certainly, it is not the only story. It is the land where I was born, quite literally "on a frosty morn" in October. That rich heritage and history of old Dixie embodies a large part of who I am. It defines me as surely as any other factor of my existence.

We Southerners are all kin, if not by blood, then certainly

by culture, but we are not stereotypes by any means. Hollywood has created Southern stereotypes, but no greater population of distinct individualists exists anywhere else in the United States. Contrary to modern media, we do not even all talk alike, nor are we any more illiterate as a whole than the rest of the nation. In fact, some of the oldest institutions of higher learning are to be found in the South. Typically, we could care less how the rest of the nation views us, for we know who we are and we know where we came from, and we are proud of that status. Because we have been silenced for so long does not mean that we have been converted. We have merely bided our time until the right opportunity arises. When that day comes, the South will rise once again and reclaim her rightful place in the history of our nation.

We may have skeletons in the closet, or senile uncles or eccentric cousins, or relatives who are labeled "different" or "touched," but when threatened, the family usually closes the circle and stands by the one experiencing problems. Our family is important in our lives, even though we may have differences of opinion, or we may disagree with another family member to the extent that sometimes there may be no communication with each other for years. In spite of this, we still consider the other as family. We will attend his or her funeral *en masse*, and spend the visitation or wake discussing the individual in question in various ways, not all of which are necessarily flattering.

Our differences from the rest of the nation are reflected in our hobbies, speech patterns, manners, and other less definable attributes. Many have tried to shed their unique Southern accents, perceiving it somehow as a form of illiteracy. A generic speech pattern seems to be the ideal. No longer do we hear the soft vowels of tidewater Virginia, or the equally soft tones of the Carolina and Georgia low country. Vanishing too are the twangs of the hill country of the Carolinas and Tennessee. Hollywood then expends considerable effort to reproduce its own idea of what a Southern accent sounds like, only to find that the result is ludicrous. What a terrible loss we have suffered in order to refute or to hide our heritage, and try to fit into a bland society of sameness. We have lost our own identity by trying to be like everyone else.

Even some of our natural Southern vegetation is different from the rest of the country.

For example, the famed Spanish moss, which is neither Spanish nor a moss that festoons the live oaks and cypresses in our coastal South once provided more than just epiphytic curtains to lend ambience to ghostly tales. The delicate gray *Tillandsia usneoides,* a bromeliad like the pineapple, that drapes its delicate tendrils from tree branches is no parasite and nor does it kill its host. Its nourishment is taken from the air. It has no roots. It grows only below the fall line, and, most importantly, below the Mason-Dixon line.

An enthusiastic Chicagoan who recently moved south, inquired as to where he might buy some Spanish moss to plant in his yard. After hearing the explanation that this particular bit of Southern flora occurs naturally and is not cultivated, and after explaining what is meant by the term "fall line," he commented in a rather bemused manner, "I guess I can just hang some in the trees then." Currently, he is busy taking note of all that is wrong with the way things operate in the small town he has chosen as his home. Predictably, he has the perfect solutions for all of the town's inherent problems. Ah, well, why am I surprised?

Native American peoples found abundant uses for Spanish moss. This intriguing plant was once harvested and used as stuffing in mattresses and in upholstered furniture. Confederate soldiers wove it into saddle blankets, and it was sometimes used to feed livestock. Others found it useful as mulch, packing materials, teas, and as an additive to strengthen mortar. Used as a tea, it was said to relieve rheumatism and diabetes. Early nineteenth century merchants exported Spanish moss to mattress factories in Europe. During the post-Depression years, more than 10,000 tons of this gray gossamer plant was harvested, cured, and ginned like cotton. This endeavor once brought more than two and half million dollars to the severely depressed South.

One often told anecdote suggests that Henry Ford quite possibly used Spanish moss as stuffing for the upholstery in his Model T. A buyer climbed in to drive away and suddenly experienced intense itching that only became more excruciating than ever as he drove. After returning the Model T to the sales office, it was discovered that chiggers or red bugs had made their home in the Spanish moss that filled the seats of the Model T. This problem was touted as Ford's first automobile recall. While the story was once widely circulated, there seems to be little basis for it, and it may be safely catalogued as another "urban legend," but it still is a good story.

In truth, the process whereby the Spanish moss was prepared for use in upholstery routinely followed a four-step procedure that included a thorough cleaning, a two-month soaking in water, being air dried in a "moss yard," and then finally baled in a mechanical gin. This method would have taken care of any insects and mites that might have found refuge in the Spanish moss. We know that such a story as that of Ford's Model T can have little basis in fact. The story remains, however, and provides a glimpse at the characteristic humor found in the South, particularly when a Yankee is involved. This is our way of coping with all the ignorant hillbilly and redneck stories that still abound. Those Yankees do not understand us, because we often do not understand ourselves, nor do we often try very hard.

A case in point is that of a man who hailed from Philadelphia. He noted that while he had lived in Savannah for nearly fifty years, one thing puzzled him and he thought someone should remedy the problem of various flags on graves in a local cemetery. In his words to a group intent on cemetery preservation, he remarked, "There are many American flags out there, a lot of Irish flags, and even some Georgia Bulldog flags. I think we ought to do away with all these flags." As the group sat somewhat spellbound, but certainly also shell shocked, the author of this book thought, "What will he think when he sees the Confederate flags on Confederate Memorial Day?" The chairman of the group hurriedly moved on to other business, thus, bypassing what would surely have become a heated discussion.

Fifteen or twenty years of living in a Southern city or town will not make you Southern. It takes at least a generation and a half, or longer, to reach the status of "native." It also helps if the Southern "wannabe" has a Confederate soldier hidden away somewhere in his family. If that should be the case, we will welcome you with open arms into our Southern culture, help you catch up on events of the last thirty years, and even introduce you to your long-lost cousins. If not, after a prescribed number of years of living in the South and hopefully absorbing its manners and mores, we may confer the currently affectionate title, "Damn Yankee" upon you. (I should warn you however, that among certain circles, a "Damn Yankee" is still used to designate a Yankee who came down here and stayed.) When that day comes, you have most definitely "arrived." If you are lucky, you may one day reach that pinnacle of social acceptance where one may say that you are truly "in high cotton." Just remember, that longevity of residence will not make you Southern. Only God's grace can do that.

There is one other symbol of the South I should mention, because it can cause visitors in our lovely cities and towns loss of sleep at night. They sometimes have the effrontery to complain about it. Not us, we wrote a song about it. Of course, human beings have a proclivity for complaining about most anything, but for some reason this small creature seriously annoys some people, particularly those who come from other places.

The mockingbird is a small gray bird with a big song in his heart. His gray coat is reminiscent of our heritage, and so is his personality. This gray warbler is most assuredly territorial, like his human counterparts, and he defends his home against all intruders and against all odds. Many a cat or dog has felt the mockingbird's wrath as he swoops down to peck an unwary tail that intruded into territory this small gray tyrant had claimed as his own personal kingdom.

In the spring and summer, when Confederate jasmine, Carolina jasmine, tea olive, and magnolias scent the air, the mockingbird sings all day, and often all night long. No music composed by man is sweeter. Yet there are those who claim their rest is disturbed by the non-stop night singing. To those I say, "Just stop and smell the magnolias, and listen to the mockingbird. Where else can one be serenaded with such mastery and fervor?" Certainly, no symphony can come close to the pure tones originating from this small Southerner. Yes, you purists, I know that he is officially referred to as the Northern mockingbird, but what's in a name?

With all these preliminaries, explanations and niceties out of the way, it is time to begin our odyssey through that lovely, lovely land called Dixie. We will stop and smell the jasmine and magnolias along the way, walk through high cotton, feel the ghostly brush of the Spanish moss against the face, and we will take a glimpse at the dark side as well. Y'all come to the land of my birth and sit a spell, and listen while I tell you a love story of the many things that make up my South, the South I dearly love. Come hear those soft Southern voices.

I Hear Bagpipes Humming

Laurinburg, North Carolina, located on the edge of a region in the Southern coastal plains known as the Sandhills, is the county seat of Scotland County, so named because of the large number of immigrants from the highlands of Scotland who came up the Cape Fear River and settled in that part of the state in the 1700s. The area, originally part of Richmond County, broke away from Richmond County in 1899 and became a separate county. The town itself took its name from the McLaurin family who were some of the early settlers in this area. Its population today is approximately 12,500 within the corporate city limits, but when I was growing up in the 1940s, there were only about 5,000 inhabitants. My parents and older brother Skippy moved here from Wilmington, North Carolina, on August 13, 1933. It would be another five years before I arrived on the scene, and my younger brother Billy would wait until 1942 to put in an appearance.

Scotland County was then an agriculturally-based community whose primary crops were corn, cotton, tobacco, watermelons, cantaloupes, and cucumbers. Some of the farmers raised small herds of beef cattle. There was a fertilizer plant that bore the name Dixie Guano, a cotton gin, a flourmill, a dairy, and a plywood plant, as well as several textile mills. We even had a community freezer locker where people could rent spaces, freeze, and store meat and vegetables, since home freezers were not common household appliances then. The grocery stores did not sell frozen foods either. That would come much later. Many of the streets were dirt, and life was fairly simple, and, for the most part, innocent. It was one of a myriad of small Southern towns where everyone, black and white, knew one another. There were a number of Lumbee Indians, or "Croatans" as they were sometimes called back then, as well. The town boasted a number of churches, around which the town's social and spiritual life centered, the usual separate schools, and a small country club, Scotch Meadows, on the outskirts of the town.

Sundays found most of the inhabitants sitting in a church of their choosing, and there were quite a few from which to choose. It was a Saturday ritual for children to polish their shoes to wear to Sunday school. Life was slower, and people were still taught to be polite and mannerly to their elders, whoever they might be. The worst thing that could possibly happen to a child who misbehaved in school was for the teacher to threaten to call one's parents. Any disciplinary measure taken at school for unacceptable behavior was sure to receive further reinforcement at home.

Children, for the most part, made their own amusements – a homemade swing suspended from a tree limb, board games, cowboys and Indians, dolls, little cars, softball, and comic books. Softball played informally, without adult supervision or coaching was also popular in the neighborhoods. It was rare indeed for adults to get involved with children's games. Childhood was for children. There were no organized sports except for the high school basketball, baseball, and football teams. Little League baseball, with its myriad cousins, was a long way down the road. Children tended to make invent their own games and establish their own rules, and these often differed from neighborhood to neighborhood. Imagination was the only prerequisite for the most popular pastimes. Recently, I read where some child experts have formed the opinion that children are not being allowed to have a childhood, because adults are over-organizing their children's lives by daily schedules of all those activities that they believe will enrich them. Children are forced to enter the adult world as soon as they begin walking. They get on the frantic treadmill early these days.

There were no public recreational facilities in Laurinburg, but a gristmill about four miles from town, at a crossroads known as X-Way, provided a small area for swimming in the cold, dark, brown cypress-stained waters of Gum Swamp. This popular swimming hole eventually closed down when a polio epidemic scare in the early 1950s seemed to indicate that the disease might be contracted from swimming areas. Concerned parents kept their offspring at home, and local health officials imposed a rather strict quarantine. The quarantine extended not only to swimming holes, but also to movies and other public places as well. During this time, children were confined to their own homes and yards.

Some mid-summer entertainments, which have all but vanished from the scene, involved certain insects that were prevalent at that time of year. One such activity involved capturing a June bug, a rather large beetle with an iridescent green shell, and tying a thread to one of its legs. This left it free to fly at the end of the thread. Why this was so entertaining is difficult to explain in modern society, but it was a source of endless amusement to chase each other with the June bug buzzing at the end of the string. When the initial thrill ended, we usually released the poor beetles. Like so many things, the June bugs are no longer as prevalent, at least not in the city.

The other activity involving insects was catching lightning bugs, or fireflies as some called them, and placing them in a fruit jar with holes punched in the lid to provide air. If a child managed to catch a large number of the bugs, they would provide a fascinating light show on warm summer nights. These small insects, like the June bugs, are not so common any more. I suppose insecticides, pollution, and loss of habitat has taken its toll on their population, or maybe we have just lost that innocent childhood wonder and don't take the time to notice their magic anymore. Rainy periods in the spring and summer frequently left numerous mud puddles along our dirt roads. We searched them diligently for tadpoles. Rare were the children who had not raised a tadpole population to the point of its metamorphoses into tiny frogs. These were later released as well. Most of us went to sleep on warm summer nights listening to the sound of the cicadas.

Saturdays were set aside for going to the movies, generally double features, which also included newsreels, and cartoons. The price of a ticket was nine cents, and a child could sit through several matinees if he was so inclined and if his parents were agreeable to the idea. Popcorn and soft drinks were not available at the picture shows in our town, but we would sometimes sneak in a candy bar in a pocket. Air conditioning had not yet found its way here. Large fans provided air circulation and some relief from the summer heat.

This was the era of young people who sat spellbound when Bela Lugosi as Dracula turned himself into a large, blood-sucking bat, when Lon Chaney sprouted facial hair and bayed at the moon, when Egyptian mummies rose up from sarcophagi to fulfill ancient curses, and Tarzan flew through the jungle on a large vine with his signature call. Other features were the westerns with Lash LaRue, Roy Rogers, Gene Autry, Hopalong Cassidy, and the Lone Ranger. There were also comedies starring The Three Stooges, Dean Martin, Jerry Lewis, Bob Hope, Bing Crosby, and others, as well as Batman and Superman adventures, cartoons, and newsreels. The love stories, war movies, and dramas were less popular among the very young, but had great appeal for the older moviegoers.

There were also traveling roller-skating rinks. Generally located in an area adjacent to Blood Field, (so-called because its shacks and shanties were often the scene of rather bloody Saturday night disturbances among its inhabitants) these portable rinks were set up under huge tents. Skates could be rented, and music was played as skaters, young and not so young, moved gracefully, or sometimes not so gracefully, around the hardwood rink. These traveling rinks would stay in town for several days, or perhaps a week, depending on the number who patronized the rink, and then the owners would take down the tent, remove the flooring, and move on to some other community.

Occasionally a traveling circus or a carnival would come to town, but this was usually in the spring or fall.

Fall was also the time of year when the country churches, particularly the Presbyterians and Methodists, held In-Gatherings. These were events where farmwives brought their pickles, preserves, pies and cakes to sell, and the men cooked and sold barbecue. The name, In-Gathering was derived from the heritage and tradition of the Scots who settled our area. Tickets for plate dinners were sold, and people ate on the church grounds. Some rural churches still continue to hold In-Gatherings, and some may still have regular dinners on the grounds after their noon service, but I suspect that these events are rare, there being no time in busy schedules to organize such things. Certainly, the few that are held bear little resemblance to that more idyllic time when mothers cooked and baked dishes to take for dinner on the grounds after church. All businesses were closed on Sundays, so there was no temptation to go shopping. As a matter of fact, many businesses also closed on Wednesday afternoons so people could attend prayer meetings at various churches on Wednesday evenings. We've come a long way, baby, but the road is not all that great, nor are the rewards that desirable in many ways. We have forgotten from whence we came.

In the late 1940s, it was a custom for both blacks and whites to go to the courthouse on an evening just before Christmas. There, on the courthouse grounds were various groups singing Christmas carols in front of a huge live Christmas tree. At the conclusion, stockings filled with oranges and candies were handed out to all the children. I only remember this occurring once or twice before the custom died out, but it was something we all looked forward to. The old courthouse is gone, razed to make room for a department store. Eventually, the department store moved to another location and the building that had replaced the old courthouse became the local Board of Education as it had outgrown its cramped offices in the old Teacherage on West Church Street.

For those who may be unfamiliar with the word, "teacherage," this term refers to a building where single female teachers who accepted a teaching position in town lived. Many Southern towns had a teacherage back then. Ours eventually fell into disuse, and the Superintendent, whose office had been located in the high school, moved his office and growing staff into the old teacherage. A law firm occupies the building now, the Board of Education offices having since moved to the second Belk building on Main Street, which became vacant when Belk moved out to the shopping center. This is our homegrown brand of recycling.

Fire protection for the county was provided by a volunteer fire department. Each resident kept a card that listed the locations of fire alarm boxes around town, as well as its call number. When a fire alarm rang, or was called in to the fire station, a loud horn, audible all over town blew in a series of blasts according to the location. For example, four short blasts followed by a pause and then four more short blasts indicated the number 44, which was the firebox in my own neighborhood. A fire call of 13, one blast and then three blasts, told the volunteers that the fire was out in the country, in which case the volunteer firemen would meet at the fire station to man the trucks and get more information about the location of the fire. Many times, the fire horn would sound during church. The men who were volunteer firemen would count the blasts of the horn, look at the card (which they carried in their pockets) listing the locations of the fire alarm box, and then quietly get up and exit the church. Unwary visitors at the Sunday services in town, would invariably ask after the conclusion of the service what that odd sound was, and why did some men get up and leave the church. Obviously, this method of calling in firemen was not the norm in other places, but it was practical and it worked. Although this method of firefighting was used up until about 1957, it was eventually replaced with more modern procedures.

The town's Main Street was approximately three blocks long. The businesses included an assortment of the usual locally owned clothing, hardware, grocery, and drug stores as well as a few chain stores such as Rose's Five and Ten, and Belk's Department Store. There were two other "dime stores" and three movie theatres. Willie Paylor's was a store that opened for an hour or two after church on Sundays so people could select from an assortment of Sunday newspapers and paperback books. Kids browsed and bought comic books there. The newspapers arrived with the mail on a train that stopped just a block up the street from Paylor's. Eidson's Shoe Repair Shop intrigued the young with its stuffed Boston Bull Terrier in the window. It was said to have been the pet of the owner who had a taxidermist mount it after the dog's death. Each of these stores had their own characteristic scents of shoe polish and leather, medicinal odors, newsprint, and in the "dime stores" (Rose's and Wood's) the fragrance of Horton's Cologne was always in evidence. Belk's was in the upper price range and carried "Evening in Paris." Even today, these scents evoke a flood of memories.

Atkinson Street in the downtown area was the site of a few businesses that are now long gone. There was located Mr. Frank McCormick's Feed Store where his granddaughter Jane McGuire and I often played in the hay bales stored there. Next door was "The Children's Shop" owned by Jane's mother. Beyond that was the office of old Dr. Caldwell, a local veterinarian, and then the offices of McNair Investment Company. The post office, with its hand painted murals of cotton fields high on the walls, was across the street. (It was there that at the tender age of three or four years I once stuck my head between the iron rails outside and got stuck. My father experienced several tense moments of pure panic as he tried to pull my head from between the rails. Just as he was considering getting a hacksaw and cutting the bars, he made one last attempt, and by folding my ears close to my head was able to extricate a crying little girl from the iron bars that held her captive). An old Victorian house that housed the police department on the ground floor and the public library on the upper floor was located just a few doors down from the post office. Laurinburg was the sort of town that when a farmer spotted the first cotton blossom on a plant, he brought it into town to the local weekly newspaper. There it was photographed and made the front page. This then was my hometown, not too far removed from Andy Griffith's fictional Mayberry.

Once when Jane and I were playing in the park in front of our respective homes, we ventured too close to some tree houses her older brother Frank, a cousin Larry, and their friend Doug had built in the park. They climbed down from their precarious perches in the tree limbs. They had tied towels around their necks, the folds billowing down their backs when they ran. They chased us down the street, claiming that they were like Superman and could fly. Convinced of the possibility that they were telling the truth, we ran into Jane's house and she called her granddaddy to come rescue us. "Mr. Frank," as we called him, came from his feed store and took both of us back there to play in the hay bales. Mr. Frank had once served as Sheriff of Scotland County, and we knew he would protect us. Ah, such youthful imagination!

These were the days when the milkman delivered the milk, fresh from the dairy, to the back door each morning. The glass milk bottles were capped with a paper cap, and the cream in the milk rose to the top. My grandmother would carefully pour off

16

the cream and save it for coffee or for whipping cream. My brother Billy would sometimes get up early and ride with the milkman on his route.

In the summer, small black children would go door-to-door selling blackberries or huckleberries, and my grandmother would always buy some to use in pies. In the fall, these same children would sell scuppernongs and muscadine grapes, both of which grew wild in nearby woods. These were made into jellies, and sometimes wine. Once Jane and I picked wild grapes growing in the park, and my mother helped us each make a small jar of jelly. We hadn't picked many, but we were so very proud of our accomplishment. I suppose this early introduction on preparing foods is the reason the South has so many great cooks. We started learning early.

Laurinburg, like many small towns across the South had its share of interesting or perhaps, eccentric characters. Mostly, these individuals were accepted as a part of the fabric of the community, and while their antics or comments might elicit a smile or two, or occasionally frustration, they were merely part of the overall fabric of small town living, and were generally accepted as such. Children who knew these individuals were non-judgmental, probably because these characters were merely part of the scene and were not regarded as being subject to intense scrutiny. They were just accepted.

One of the more colorful of these local characters was Johnny Covington. The Laurinburg & Southern Railroad, a branch of the Seaboard Railroad that ran from Charlotte to Wilmington, had several daily trains. The old train depot at the end of North Main Street was a rather busy place in the early 1940s. The trains brought the mail into town, and usually when a train was due to arrive, many of the townspeople were there to watch it come in.

Johnny Covington was one such person. No one seems to agree on whether or not Johnny had actually worked for the railroad, but at some point in his life, he had acquired a train conductor's cap and jacket. In the 1940s, trains on the Eastern Seaboard Railroad passed through Laurinburg several times a day on their journey between Hamlet to the west and Wilmington to the east. The trains brought the mail, and Johnny was always around to meet the trains. He also hung around the post office. People would drive up to mail letters. Johnny would walk up to their car, where they would hand him the letters to mail and also a small coin or two. Johnny was somewhat of a local celebrity in his own mind, and he took his responsibilities seriously. He never failed to place the letter in the proper mail slot.

Johnny Covington

His home was upstairs at the B. Morris Funeral Home on Roper Street, the funeral home that served the surrounding black community. It was upstairs that the bodies awaiting

18

burial were kept, and it was here that Johnny slept, surrounded by the dead. When questioned as to whether it bothered him to sleep up there with the dead folks, his surprising reply, for that era at least, was that dead folks were dead and were not going to bother anyone. This was a somewhat enlightened observation, considering the prevalence of superstitions among both the black and white population at that time.

At one point in his life, Johnny had a run-in with the law, which resulted in his serving a sentence at the County Farm. Many of the inmates incarcerated there were used on work details, especially during cotton-picking time. Johnny, upon arrival at the Farm, was quick to inform authorities there that he had his own ideas about this practice. In no uncertain terms, he told them, "I didn't plant no cotton, an' I ain't pickin' no cotton!" Johnny's sentence was served in the kitchen at the Farm.

Johnny went to his rest in 1977 at the age of 72. His remains were buried at Cedar Grove Cemetery in Laurinburg. A plain granite marker includes, along with his name, birth, and death dates, the simple inscription: "Free Spirit – Friend To All." He rests beside his sister.

Another interesting character that I remember was Garfield, an old Negro man who lived not far from our house near a place we called the Sand Pit. Exactly how the Sand Pit came into being, I do not remember ever hearing, but it was probably a small, shallow "borrow pit" where someone in need of sand "borrowed" it. It was a place children were warned to avoid. It seems that several young boys once decided to dig a cave into the side of the very large mound of the sand. They dug rather too deep. The cave collapsed, burying one of the boys. Garfield heard the screams of the other boys and came to the rescue. He managed to dig out the boy who had been buried by the collapse of the sand into the cave. I do not remember whether the boy survived, but I do remember my daddy telling us that Garfield was a hero. While I was not sure exactly what a hero was, I was nevertheless impressed by this title.

Today, the appellate "hero" is used carelessly for even the most insignificant events and has thus been robbed of any real meaning. In the era of which I speak, the term "hero" was only applied to designate someone who rendered aid to someone in extreme circumstances in a life-threatening situation. It was never applied to a victim. Today's careless use of the term has robbed it of its true significance, and the word has become meaningless. Today everybody is a hero. I have yet to figure out why. Why is it heroic to have a good report card, for heaven's sakes! It is highly commendable and laudable to overcome some handicap or unusual crisis, but such achievements, while worthy of note and praise, hardly merit someone being called a hero.

There were always books in our house. My father was a voracious reader and a true bibliophile in every sense of the word. He bought books that interested him, and was a regular patron of the small public library. In the evenings, he always had a stack of books beside his favorite chair. My grandmother loved poetry, particularly that of such poets as Henry Wadsworth Longfellow and Oliver Wendell Holmes from whom she claimed lineal descent. She was also an avid reader of Sidney J. Harris, a syndicated poet whose verses appeared regularly in the daily newspaper. These verses she clipped and carefully kept to paste into a scrapbook. In addition to the poems, she faithfully worked the crossword puzzle in the paper each morning. She usually had a jigsaw puzzle in progress on a card table in her bedroom. My mother devoted herself to reading the newspaper and to reading poetry as well. All of the adults read to the children in the household. Of course, reading the Bible was strongly encouraged.

With the saturation of books, and exposure to various literary pursuits in our house, it is not surprising that my two brothers and I sought avocations in writing. My older brother Skippy was always writing stories, but did not live long enough to publish any. My younger brother Billy did study journalism at the University of North Carolina, and did pursue a successful career in investigative newspaper work. He had begun working on a promising novel, which a professor at Chapel Hill thought had merit. It dealt with the North Carolina textile industry and the attempts to establish unions in the mid-1900s in North Carolina. He continued working on it as his job at the newspaper permitted. His premature death halted that endeavor, and I suppose the unfinished manuscript lies slowly yellowing and gathering dust in a forgotten box somewhere.

My father was also a music lover. Although he did not play a musical instrument, he decided that I would be the musician in the family. Accordingly, when I was barely five years old, he arranged for me to take piano lessons with Mrs. Elizabeth Yongue who lived just a block from our house. I regularly trudged down the dirt street to Mrs. Yongue's home and learned to read the music and the corresponding keys on the piano. My first and only opportunity to appear on the stage as a child prodigy of great talent came when I appeared in my first piano recital.

The recital was held at an elementary school in the little

21

town of Wagram, about ten miles from Laurinburg. My mother had made a beautiful pink evening dress for me to wear. My father, bursting with pride, saw that I had a corsage to wear. My grandmother arranged my hair in curly ringlets. I am sure that I felt like a princess that night.

My first piano recital

I had memorized a piece of music called *The Brook*, and I waited anxiously backstage for my turn to perform. Finally, my turn arrived and I walked out on the stage to the piano with the sort of confidence known only to the very young. I began to play *The Brook* in what was without a doubt a flawless and stellar performance. As I stood up, faced the audience and curtsied, they burst into applause.

22

With such an obvious indication that an encore was in order, I sat back down at the piano and played *The Brook* once more. Again, the sound of applause reached my ears, an intoxicating sound, and so, once again, I played *The Brook*. By this time, my father who was seated on the front row and who had beamed at my first encore began to fidget somewhat. No doubt, there were numerous titters among the audience. When I began my fourth encore, my father had half risen from his seat when Mrs. Yongue walked out on the stage, took me by the hand, and led me away as once more the applause sounded. Ah, but applause is so intoxicating!

Meanwhile backstage, Mrs. Yongue's son Douglas, who was to follow me on the program, had waited impatiently for his opportunity to perform. Being upstaged by a little uninhibited five-year-old girl was no doubt annoying to say the least. His moment of glory had been pre-empted, and while he was applauded after his own performance at the piano, he did not get the encores I received. Ah, such is fame! And so fleeting.

Other piano recitals followed that premier performance, but none of them ever elicited the pride I felt at that very first one. As I grew older and continued to take piano lessons until I was a junior in high school, I realized that talent and mechanical skill are two entirely different matters altogether, and that I fell into the mechanical group rather than possessing any natural talent. My interest in playing waned, although the love of music remained.

Two blocks from our house, just inside the limits of Carolina Park, stood an old two-story frame house. I was very, very young when the house caught fire one night. My daddy woke me up and allowed me to go with him to the fire. The volunteer fire department came, but the house was so old it could not be saved and it burned to the ground. Within a day or two, rumors began circulating that a woman had died in the fire. According to our maid, the body of a woman was found

23

kneeling beside what had been a bed. Upon examination of the charred remains, a large old-fashioned hatpin had been driven into her forehead. This was a topic of conversation around our house for some time. If the matter was ever given credence by a police investigation, it was never discussed in my hearing.

Prince Street, which ran beside our house, was a dirt road in the early 1940s. It was located in a subdivision known at that time as Quinn Marshall. In front of our house was Park Circle and across the street was The Park. In later years, it was formally called Hammond Park. Prince Street was a rather heavily traveled street. A road-scraper, which came on a fairly regular basis, kept the road relatively smooth of ruts most of the time. I remember when sewer lines became clogged, how the city would send a crew out to dig up the streets to unclog them. Often this work took several days, so barricades were put up around the hole and round kerosene burners or smudge pots were placed by the barricades and lighted so that no unsuspecting vehicle would run into the hole left by the excavation. Of course, all such roadwork was thoroughly supervised by the neighborhood children who played on the scrapers, and other heavy equipment after the workers got off work at night. In the summer, the dusty road was sprayed periodically with oil from a city truck to keep the dust down. Environmentalists would have a stroke if such a remedy were suggested today.

Carolina Park, a black neighborhood, was located along Prince Street, just two blocks past our house. Old Dan Monroe used to pass this way, driving his mule and wagon. He would sometimes allow me to climb up on the back of his wagon and ride with him for a block or two. He referred to me as "Miss Darfy." Dan ran a little store in Carolina Park, and all of the neighborhood children patronized it, especially in the summertime when he did a booming business in five-cent Coca Colas, Pepsis, and Nehi Colas. He had some competition from another resident of Carolina Park by the name of Estelle. She also operated a little store just a few doors away from Dan's, and was a more serious businesswoman. While Dan would occasionally slip an extra piece of penny candy to us, Estelle never did. We usually alternated our patronage, so that both storekeepers got some of our business.

Another frequent traveler along this street was a tall, thin black woman named Hela. Hela's distinctive trademark was the snow-white turban she wore on her head. That, combined with her erect, regal bearing and very dark skin, only added to her mysterious demeanor. She never seemed to speak to anyone or to acknowledge anyone with even a nod. Many of the Negro inhabitants were afraid of Hela. She had a reputation for being a conjure woman, and, thus, was a person other people felt was best left alone. She managed to convey a mysterious aloofness that few dared to question. There finally came a time when we no longer saw Hela walking down the road. She had disappeared, and no one seemed to know where she had gone. Eventually, her absence ceased to cause comment, and she became a distant memory, only resurrected when someone told scary stories.

One of the more interesting persons who may have inhabited Carolina Park, if only briefly, was the infamous James Diggs. Wanted for the cold-blooded murder of a police officer in the little town of Hamlet, he was the subject of an intense manhunt. The search took on special significance due to the fact that the police officer's brother lived in Laurinburg. It was believed that Diggs had relatives living in Carolina Park and that he might try to make his way there seeking family members to hide him. The children in our neighborhood were transfixed as a procession of police cars made a speedy trip down Prince Street on a sunny afternoon, heading for Carolina Park. We stood on the side of the street looking in the direction they had gone. We learned that Diggs had been placed on the Ten Most Wanted list by the F.B.I.

Frank McGuire, who was about a year older than I was,

25

voiced his concerns that James Diggs, in trying to escape the law, might try to steal his horse, which was kept in the McGuire's backyard. We children were all in agreement that this was a legitimate concern. To thwart such an escape attempt, Frank got his horse and led it into the front yard. He then proceeded to try to coax the horse up the steps into the screened porch. As he struggled with the reluctant horse, Frank's mother intervened and made him take the horse back to the stable in their backyard. Not to be discouraged, Frank decided that if he painted the buggy that the horse was often hitched to, then James Diggs would not be able to use that as a means of transportation, because the wet paint would be a deterrent to its use. Problem solving began at an early age.

James Diggs vanished, and was never captured as far as I am aware. I do know that when I was a high school senior on our senior trip to Washington, D.C., we toured the F.B.I. building there. As we looked at the list of the Ten Most Wanted, there was James Diggs' name on the list.

World War II affected the lives of many people here. Although I was probably three or four years old at the time, I have a vivid memory of blackouts and of planes flying over the darkened town. Daddy served as an air raid warden whose duty it was to make sure that everyone turned their lights off and kept their windows covered so that enemy planes flying over could not spot a target. German submarines were reported to be in the waters off the North Carolina coast, especially in the area around Wilmington. My older brother Skippy wanted to join the Navy, and because of his age, Daddy had to sign permission in order for him to enlist. He was sent to the Hawaiian Islands where he manned a radio shack on a mountainside with an intelligence unit. Because of security measures, the letters he sent back home were censored with a heavy black pen. We were to learn much later that he was posted in the mountains of Hawaii, not far from Pearl Harbor. While operating a radio there, he received the ticker tape that brought the message of the surrender ceremonies aboard the USS *Missouri* in Tokyo Bay on September 2, 1945. Japanese officials signed the documents of surrender on the deck of "Big Mo," which were received and accepted by General Douglas MacArthur.

We were given a small red-bordered flag with a single blue star set in the center of a white background. Mother hung the flag in the window to show that we had a family member in service. The number of stars denoted the number of servicemen from each family that received such a flag. The Laurinburg-Maxton Air Base was a glider base, and large numbers of soldiers came into town, some bringing their families. Because of the lack of sufficient housing, many people rented extra rooms in their homes to house the soldier's families. Gasoline and sugar were rationed, and stamps were issued for these items. Scrap metal was collected and sent to distribution centers where it was then sent to factories to be recycled into war materials.

Even pets were involved in the patriotic efforts. "Boots," Skippy's American bulldog who could be counted upon to produce a large litter of nondescript puppies with alarming regularity, had a litter of pups that resembled German shepherds. The pups had been given away to various people in town. One of them, "Wolfie," had a penchant for instigating problems, the most notable of which was once when he attacked a pig belonging to a Negro man in Carolina Park. "Wolfie" had the pig, which was screaming loudly, securely by the ear. "Boots," in her efforts to aid "Wolfie," killed the pig. Daddy made appropriate financial restitution to the pig's owner. At any rate, "Wolfie" was given to an owner who donated the dog to the war effort. "Wolfie" became a member of the K-9 Corps. He was eventually discharged and returned home with his master at the end of the war. Wolfie spent his remaining days lying on the sidewalk in front of his owner's barbershop.

It was during this period that I contracted scarlet fever, which resulted in a quarantine notice being posted on our front door by the county health department. A number of army doctors from the air base came to see me because many of them had never encountered scarlet fever. Mercifully, my baby brother Billy did not come down with the disease, and I eventually recovered with no lasting effects.

The end of the war brought additional changes to the town. The soldiers returned home. Some soldiers, who were stationed near here, or at the Laurinburg-Maxton glider base, stayed and found a place for themselves in the community. Skippy came home and went back to college. Daddy died suddenly, and life, with all of its vagaries, went on. Skippy would die of heart disease a year later at the age of 22, and thus, our lives would once again change when Mother went to work for the American Red Cross as Executive Director, a post she would hold for more than forty years. My paternal grandmother, who was living with us, took care of us after school.

Our pleasures were simple in those long-gone days. Television was nonexistent, and organized sports and activities were in the future. We created our own entertainment, and if we were deprived, no one thought to tell us about it. In happy, blissful ignorance we pursued our own interests, going to school, making up games, climbing trees, reading comic books, playing cards, dolls, toy cars, and storytelling. Occasionally, my mother would put us all in the car and take us to a drive-in movie.

Most people in town had heard the story of how old John F. McNair, who had enlisted in the 18th North Carolina Troops, walked all the way home from Appomattox Courthouse with only a rifle to his name. He managed to acquire a mule, which he hitched to a plow and set about establishing a farm. By acquiring more land and putting in more crops, he eventually established himself as the wealthiest man in the county, especially since he owned most of it. By the time the third generation of McNairs came into their own, the family owned much of the county, a number of businesses, a dairy, McNair Feed and Seed Store, Pioneer Seed Company, and McNair Investment Corporation. Everyone knew that the McNairs were Scotland County.

On summer evenings, after supper (dinner was always the meal in the middle of the day), people who had porches sat out at night and children played in the yard with friends. Often we sat with parents and neighbors and listened to the stories they would sometimes relate with a little urging from the young avid listeners. The really juicy gossip was never discussed within the hearing distance of the young audience. However, we somehow always managed to be within earshot if the conversation seemed to be deemed unfit for young ears. My mother's favorite expression was "Little pitchers have big ears." I once overhead my mother and one of her friends talking about some woman who had "V. D." When I innocently asked what V.D. was, my mother replied without missing a beat, "Vitamin Deficiency." It was on occasions such as these that I first heard the stories, which I now relate.

It was truly an age of innocence for many of us. Life seemed to plod along in a dreamy sort of way in the 1940s and 1950s. Changes taking place in other parts of the country or overseas, had little obvious effect on our small town existence. While other Southern urban areas were somewhat ahead of the small towns, they too were deliberate in making any real changes in their way of life. Even now, as I look back, there was a sort of surreal quality about the way we went about our ordinary lives. Life still moved slowly here in the South, even in the cities. We were still Southern, and were not too concerned about cosmopolitan pursuits.

Italian "Spaghetti," Southern Style

I was in the fifth or sixth grade at Central School when I first learned about "Spaghetti," a mummified Italian man who was kept in a case at the local funeral home a block from the school. Several of my classmates and many of the older students had talked about seeing the mummy, thus kindling my imagination and intense desire to see this creepy, legendary figure. Accordingly, I walked home from school that afternoon with one or two of my friends who had already viewed the mummy, choosing a route that passed by the funeral home. The garage door to the funeral home was open that afternoon, revealing the two hearses kept there. My friends led me into the garage, and there fastened to the left-hand wall near one of the hearses was a narrow wooden cabinet hanging on the wall. One of my companions reached up, lifted the simple latch that held the cabinet door closed, and opened the door.

Inside the door, a full length glass pane separated the viewer from the viewee... a very tall, at least to my childish mind, dark brown figure of a man, clad only in a loincloth, hanging inside the cabinet by a rope which passed under his arms and fastened somewhere at the back of the cabinet. His hands were crossed at the groin area, which was modestly covered by a loincloth. The skin, which was leathery-looking, was stretched tautly over his skeletal frame. The most startling feature however, was the teeth that gleamed whitely against the darkened face. I stared at the figure with macabre fascination. As I continued to stand there, I noticed what appeared to be a large wooden club in the lower right corner of the case. In the other corner was a mummified fetus. My eyes kept stealing upward to those horrifying white teeth on the main character. Those teeth had a hypnotic appeal, especially to a young, impressionable mind.

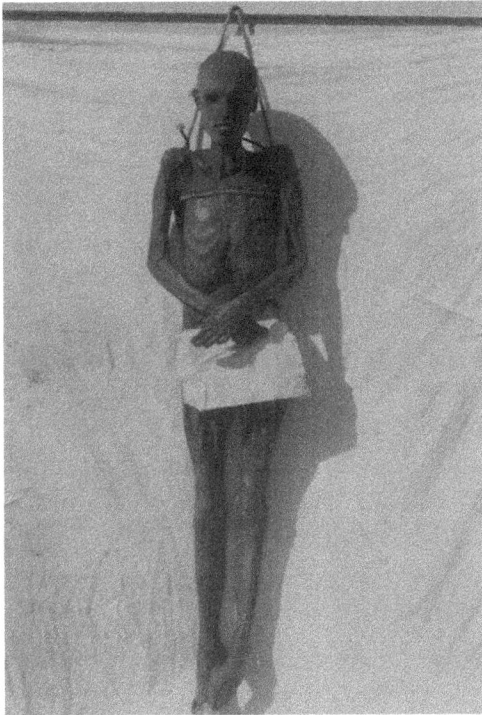

Spaghetti

Later that evening, I mentioned my visit to the funeral home, but my mother made little comment, other than to say that she hoped I had satisfied my curiosity. That night when I turned out the light in my bedroom, in my mind's eye I could still see those gleaming white teeth. That sight was to haunt my sleep for weeks to come. I vowed never to set my eyes on that nightmarish object again, a vow that I did not keep for I returned to view the mummy several times after that. I heard various classmates talk about some students hiding a microphone near the case and transmitting various messages – "Let me out of here!" or, "I'm going to get you!" – for the benefit of the unwary visitor. This stunt was most effective around Halloween.

Laurinburg's dubious tourist attraction owed its origins in an even smaller town, McColl, just across the state line in South Carolina. It was there that a traveling carnival came in 1911. Two of the workers had a dispute over a woman, a dispute that ended when one of the workers picked up one of the large wooden tent pegs and killed the other with a blow to the head. The victim was a young man of Italian descent by the name of Cancetto Farmica. He was 23 years old at the time.

The victim was taken to Laurinburg, which had the nearest hospital, but the unfortunate Farmica was dead. The murderer escaped, and the circus hurriedly packed up and left town. No real inquest or indictment was part of the legal process in this instance. A relative of Farmica's came to Laurinburg and gave a small amount of money to the undertaker, promising to return with the balance. Time passed and no one came forth to pay the undertaker for his services for embalming the corpse. Burial could not take place because no one claimed the body.

For more than fifty years, the corpse of Cancetto Farmica slowly mummified until it was little more than a husk of dark brown leather stretched tightly over its skeleton. Eventually, a wooden cabinet case was built to hold the mummy. Out of town visitors, people just passing through, or curious locals, would make McDougald Funeral Home's macabre occupant, an attraction not to be missed. The name "Spaghetti" was given to the mummy, since no one knew his name or else could not pronounce it, but it was known that he was Italian and spaghetti was an Italian word, wasn't it? From time to time, various groups would raise objections at making a human corpse a tourist attraction.

A tourist from up North once approached Mr. Hewitt McDougald, owner of the funeral home, and offered to buy

"Spaghetti." The tourist planned to exhibit the mummy for a time and then have a burial. Mr. McDougald, who was known for his dry wit, indicated that he would be willing to sell "Spaghetti." When asked what price he would be asking, Mr. McDougald replied, "one dollar a day storage for 356 days for 60 years." Needless, to say, the prospective buyer declined. The last time I had occasion to view the mummy was in the late 1960s when I took my husband-to-be to see our main attraction. Eventually, a man of Italian lineage sent a sum of money to the funeral home for the burial of "Spaghetti." That, combined with donations from local citizens, became a minor media event.

Mr. McDougald provided the body with a suit and a casket, and a public burial was planned. On September 30, 1972, a large crowd gathered at Hillside Cemetery in Laurinburg to attend the interment of a man who for sixty-one years had been Laurinburg's star tourist attraction. A short formal service was held and the casket lowered into the grave. A cement mixer then filled the grave with cement in order to deter vandalism of the grave. A bronze marker set in a rectangular granite base marks the grave. The inscription simply reads:

CANCETTO FARMICA
DIED APRIL 28, 1911
AGE 23 YEARS
BURIED SEPT. 30, 1972

Today, a casual passerby or visitor may linger briefly to read the inscription. He may pause for a moment to wonder why the burial of this person took place sixty-two years after his death. Only by talking to some of the older residents will he hear this strange story. It is likely that many of the younger generation have never heard of "Spaghetti" who made such a lasting impression on those impressionable youths of an earlier time.

Certainly, they never had the opportunity to gaze upon the mummy and experience the accompanying nightmares that were inflicted on an earlier generation after such a viewing. All that remains of this attraction is the enigmatic inscription on a bronze foot marker at Hillside Cemetery.

CANCETTO FARMICA
DIED APRIL 28, 1911
AGE 23 YEARS
BURIED SEPT. 30, 1972

Spaghetti's Grave Marker

Those Intrepid Ladies

The colorful or the eccentric characters that were nearly always in evidence were not confined to a particular race or gender. Some of our female citizens were every bit as fascinating as the ones previously mentioned.

Any child growing up in the 1940s and 1950s in Laurinburg knew and had heard the stories of our confirmed kleptomaniac, Miss Tillie Rivenbark, a rather delicate looking lady who roamed the town day and night. Although known to be quite well-to-do, and the owner of a number of rental properties, nevertheless, she collected a variety of items from the unsuspecting and uninformed. The stories of her digging up azaleas which had been newly-planted on lots at the cemetery, stealing a small marble stone because she needed it to make pulled mints on, and her collection of single shoes and gloves obtained from unnamed sources, could not compete with her greatest triumph, however.

It seems that Miss Tillie once traveled to Wilmington, North Carolina, where she also owned property. At that time, one of Wilmington's streets was broad with a wide median that contained numerous plantings and fountains decorated with large iron frogs weighing a considerable amount. Miss Tillie must have admired those iron frogs greatly, for when morning arrived, one of the frogs was missing from the fountain. Careful detective work led authorities to Miss Tillie's door. Sure enough, there was the missing frog. It took three strong city workers to take the frog and restore it to the fountain. Miss Tillie had managed the task all by herself. The adage that where there is a will, there is a way, was certainly proved correct. Our Southern ladies are no wimps.

Perhaps it is pointless to note that in spite of all of her escapades, Miss Tillie never ran into serious problems with the legal system. Potential victims were all well aware of her somewhat strange proclivities and took the proper precautions. In the case of a local grocer, these precautions included a quick search of her belongings before she left the store. When contraband was found, it was quietly confiscated and returned to its proper shelf in the store. There was no compelling desire to prosecute. After all, she was one of us.

And yet, with all of her propensity for "acquiring" things, Miss Tillie was a well-mannered lady and quite genteel. She played the piano beautifully, and according to her nearest neighbors, they were sometimes awakened late at night to beautiful piano concertos and sonatas drifting on the evening breeze from Miss Tillie's house.

I suppose that at some point in Miss Tillie's life, there had been a Mr. Rivenbark, but he had passed away long before we knew her. Local children were told that Miss Tillie had a son, but he was evidently grown and did not live in our town. No doubt, she was a lonely old lady. Sometimes young teenagers who were fond of roaming around late at night, especially at Halloween, would come upon Miss Tillie intent on her furtive missions around town. Today, her nocturnal ramblings would not be prudent in view of the sad state of our society, but in those days of innocence, she was quite safe from those who would do her harm.

Another memorable lady in our town was Miss Annie B. Stewart. Annie B. lived on the outskirts of town, out in the country. I only remember seeing her when she would come into town to do her grocery shopping. Southern ladies have an affinity with hats, and Annie B. was the proud possessor of many beautiful hats. When she came into town, she always wore one of her legendary hats. They were impressive. The only jarring note to her attire was the pair of tennis shoes she wore with her dresses and hats.

Annie B. once had the opportunity to go to California to visit a close relative who had prospered in the environs of Hollywood. While in California, Annie B. attended a party given by the well-known movie director, John Ford. Her moment of glory arrived when she was introduced to the movie actor, John Wayne, who kissed her cheek. It was rumored later that Annie B. never washed that cheek again. We were mightily impressed by the fact that this was a lady who had met John Wayne in person. His kissing her was icing on the cake as far as we were concerned.

I should probably insert a note here concerning the various maiden ladies in our town, and the Southern practice of referring to such ladies as "Miss." This designation for maiden ladies is no longer in fashion anymore, but to those who grew up in the 1930s, 1940s and 1950s, it was second nature to address such ladies as "Miss." While the term "Aunt" or "Auntie" may have been used for older black ladies in some places, my friends and I usually addressed them as "Miss" also, as in Miss Annie Washington who lived in Carolina Park.

The principal of the white grammar or elementary school in Laurinburg was Miss Kate McIntyre. All of her students and their parents referred to her only as "Miss Kate." I was probably in the sixth grade before I became aware that Miss Kate had a surname. She was never called "Miss McIntyre" by anyone I knew. She was always "Miss Kate."

Miss Kate had a sister, Miss Carrie who taught a Sunday school class at the Presbyterian Church. She was famous for the wonderful cakes she made and brought to the dinner on the grounds, an event that occurred at the church periodically. Her caramel cakes were legendary.

The other Sunday school teacher to receive this designation was Miss Roberta Coble. She was always called "Miss Roberta." She had once taught school, and her former students still referred to her as "Miss Roberta." Everyone knew Miss Roberta.

Along with the use of "Miss" for certain older ladies, regardless of their marital status, there were two other phrases heard frequently back then. One was the expression, "I swanny," to denote mild disbelief or to simply express amazement. "Bless her (or his) heart" was also heard fairly often in conversations. For example, one might hear something like this in casual conversation, "I swanny, if Joe, bless his heart, don't look just like his daddy!" "Poor Mary, bless her heart, worked hard all of her life." While the expression, "I swanny" is seldom heard much today, one may still hear "bless his (or her) heart" injected into sentences uttered by members of an older generation.

School and church were closely entwined, and what was learned at school was carried over to the Sunday school and church. The reverse was also true. Although the city school system did not receive funds for Bible studies, the local churches in our town hired a Bible teacher who came into our classrooms in the elementary school on a regular weekly schedule. It was part of our curriculum and everyone in our town felt it to be an important part of our education. We did not question the practice. It was part of going to school and was accepted as such. Nobody ever complained about it.

Before I move on to other matters, this is probably a good point to briefly mention a common practice of these bygone days – that of Girl Scouts selling red poppies on Veterans' Day, November 11th. People still talked about the Great War, otherwise known as World War I. On this day, Girl Scouts were given bundles of red artificial poppies with small tags attached to the stems. The girls stood on the streets in front of businesses and the post office asking for donations for veterans. There was no set price, but whatever a person contributed entitled them to wear a red poppy in their lapel. I cannot recall anyone refusing to contribute. The money was turned over to the American Legion.

The red poppy symbolized soldiers who were killed in the trenches of World War I, many of whom slept in the French cemetery in Flanders. The emblem was chosen from a well-known poem by Canadian soldier John McCrae who wrote, "In Flanders fields, the poppies blow between the crosses row on row that mark their place. While in the sky, the larks still bravely fly..." Most schools observed Veterans' Day by holding special programs, during which at some point this poem was always read. Indeed, most schoolchildren knew the poem by heart. This nice custom has seemingly died out, probably because there are few if any World War I veterans still living. It was a way of remembering and recognizing sacrifices our soldiers made for their country.

These were the days, when weekly assemblies were held in the school auditorium to the delight of the children who got a break in the classroom routine. Students lined up at their classroom door and marched into the auditorium to designated seats. The music teacher played marches on the piano during this time, usually *Anchors Aweigh!*, *Clayton's Grand March*, or perhaps, a Sousa march. It was rather nice to march into the auditorium keeping time to the music. Many of the programs presented had a patriotic theme, unless a particular holiday was approaching. Plays and skits were also part of the program. Occasionally we had a speaker from the community.

At Christmas, there was always a religious program which included a manger scene with Joseph, Mary, and the infant Jesus. Nobody was ever offended by these practices. It was just the norm in our small world.

The Irreverent Reverend

My interest in old cemeteries is inherited from my mother who loved to walk among the forgotten graves in old cemeteries and read the quaint inscriptions. One of the places we visited on several occasions was the old Stewartsville Cemetery, a Scottish burial ground just a few miles from town. The old cemetery is filled with a large number of immigrants from the Isle of Skye in Scotland. The origin of the people buried there is written on the stones themselves... "Born on the Isle of Skye...Islay...Coll...Appin" and so on. There were Stewarts there, and McQueens, McLaurins, McKenzies, McKinnons, and many more, most of whose names began with "Mac" or "Mc." One grave, however, was always singled out for a more detailed explanation. It was that of a man named Colin Lindsay, an itinerant preacher.

According to local tradition, this man was born several years after his mother had died and was buried. (Perhaps it is appropriate to mention here that in Scotland County at least, the Scottish name Colin was always pronounced "Kō'-lin," with a long "o"; not the short "ŏ" as pronounced in "Collin." The pronunciation of other local names were different from those in other parts; for example, the name McEachin was pronounced "McCann," and the town of Fayetteville forty miles to the north was pronounced by most locals as "Fedville." You may still hear that pronunciation among the older set.)

The story of Colin Lindsay begins on the island of Arran in Scotland. The year was 1738. Mrs. Lindsay was very ill with one of the numerous diseases that plagued 18th century Europe. Medical knowledge at that period relied on experimental treatments, herbs, leeches, and various remedies concocted either by the doctors themselves or by the apothecaries.

The Entrance to Stewartsville Cemetery

The accounts of what transpired are rather sketchy, but most agree that Mrs. Lindsay lapsed into a coma and apparently died. Her body was placed in a coffin and buried in a tomb in the local burial ground. One version calls it a burial vault. At any rate, that night, grave robbers opened the grave and lifted out the coffin, which they then opened. Mrs. Lindsay had been buried with several pieces of jewelry, one of which was a ring. One of the grave robbers tried to pull the ring from the "corpse's" finger, but the ring would not come off. The grave robber then pulled out a knife for cutting off the "corpse's" finger in order to get the ring. He had barely cut the skin when the "corpse" moaned and moved, and eventually sat up. The grave robbers fled the site, frightened beyond belief. Mrs. Lindsay then climbed out of the coffin and walked the short distance to her house. Inside the house, the grieving Mr. Lindsay was sitting with friends when footsteps were heard at the door. "That sounds like my wife's footsteps," he said. The door was opened, and there stood Mrs. Lindsay, still in her burial garments.

Several years later, in 1744, a son, Colin, was born. He grew up to become a minister and immigrated to America to preach the Gospel. Descriptions of the Reverend Colin Lindsay reveal him as a handsome man of superior intellect and ability, as well as one who had little patience for those who disagreed with him. He arrived in North Carolina about 1795, and came to the area that would much later be known as Scotland County. There he established a reputation for himself as one of the area's more colorful characters.

Records of the Presbyterian Church indicate that the Rev. Colin Lindsay was overly fond of spirits, (the liquid kind) and was reprimanded on several occasions by the church elders and the governing body of the Presbytery. Accounts of his conflicts as a minister of Orange Presbytery in the Synod of North Carolina indicate that the Rev. Lindsay held rather strong opinions on a number of topics and was not afraid to expound on any of them. According to *The Lumber River Scots* by Rev. Edwin Purcell, the Reverend Lindsay "not only advocated the right to indulge in liquors, but made no concealment of the fact that he indulged himself whenever he felt like it." This view eventually earned Lindsay a suspension from the Presbytery for excessive drinking.

The Rev. Lindsay was a vehement opponent of the so-called "Great Revival Movement" that began in the early 1800s in America He referred to that particular movement as "the work of the Devil." The concept of the jerking body, the speaking in "tongues," the wailing, swooning, and other characteristics which marked the revival movement, was abhorrent to a man steeped in the more conservative and dignified traditional form of worship inherent in the Scottish kirk. At a meeting of the Presbytery in 1803, Rev. Lindsay, when called to task regarding his views on revivals, responded to queries as to whether he believed any members of his church would attend a camp meeting replied, "I think not, for I have advised them not to come or to go to any such meeting." A witness reported that Lindsay claimed that a revival was a "delusion of the Devil."

Colin Lindsay died December 1, 1817, at the age of 73. Lindsay was a man who like many of his era believed in keeping his affairs in order, so it was no surprise to find that he had made a will in which he left everything he owned, primarily 1,000 acres of land in Robeson, Richmond, and Cumberland counties, to his beloved wife Elizabeth McLaughlin Lindsay. Upon her death, the estate would go to Lindsay's favorite nephew, Colin McLaughlin.

Reverend Lindsay was buried in the old Stewartsville Cemetery, and a simple stone was erected on his grave. The inscription gives no hint of his auspicious beginnings. It merely reads:

IN
Memory of the
Rev. Colin Lindsay
Who died
Decr. 1st 1817
In the 73rd year
of his age.

Stewartsville Cemetery has been neglected over the many years that span its existence. Though there have been a number of attempts to clean up its unkempt appearance and reset some of the fallen stones, the site is still a place where vandalism and litter are a major problem. A fence surrounds the cemetery, but it is not much of a deterrent to those who take pleasure in destroying and trashing old graveyards. Descendants of these early settlers have replaced some of the old, badly damaged stones with modern granite ones. County officials generally neglect this valuable genealogical and historical site.

In 1955, a Scotland County native, Nettie McCormick Henley, wrote an account of her family and her childhood in the southern part of the county. Her people were Highland Scots who came to America in the early 1800s. They settled in Scotland County, a few miles out in the country from Laurinburg.

A chapter in her book, *The Homeplace*, tells of an old Negro man who apparently died while sitting in his chair. By the time his body was discovered and taken away to the funeral home, rigor mortis prevented him from lying flat in his coffin. The undertaker used ropes to tie the corpse flat in the coffin. During the funeral, while the preacher was delivering the eulogy, the restraining rope snapped, releasing the stiffened body, which suddenly sat up in the coffin. The startled preacher leaped across the coffin and ran outside, followed by a large portion of the gathered mourners. Presumably, sanity soon prevailed and the corpse was decently buried.

While there were no doubt cases of actual premature burials in the days before modern medical practices made such occurrences extremely rare and modern embalming techniques render this highly unlikely today, reported incidents of such burials taking place were mostly fiction. The theme of the premature burial of individuals who later revived and re-entered society was a popular literary device dating from the early 1700s. By the Victorian era, death was a primary topic for writers, such as Edgar Allan Poe, and elaborate customs dealing with all phases of dying became entrenched in the Victorian society. These customs included not only the etiquette of death such as dress, jewelry, letters edged in black, and others, but also safety devices such as bells or flags that were used to connect the casket and its occupant with the outside world to notify friends and relative that the corpse was in fact very much alive. While such practices were not widespread, these practices were responsible of introducing new phrases, "saved by the bell," "graveyard shift," and others, into common usage. Today these expressions are regularly used without the speaker thinking about what they originally meant.

The idea of a person being born after his or her mother was declared dead, buried or entombed, and then subsequently being revived was a common theme in literature. Thus are legends born. Such is the case of the legendary premature burial of Anne Hill Carter Lee, mother of that great icon of Southern history, Robert Edward Lee. This myth is believed to have been fabricated by a Kentucky man who claimed to be a cousin of Robert E. Lee.

An old scrapbook from a now defunct Chapter of the United Daughters of the Confederacy® contained a newspaper story relating to Mrs. Lee's premature burial glued to a page. Unfortunately, the article had been trimmed to fit the page, and therefore no masthead or date was on the paper. The article, based on the other dates, which are on some pages, appears to have been published in the early 1930s. It refers to the following story and was claimed to be "authenticated" by virtue of its having been found in a scrapbook belonging to a UDC member. The story was presented at a meeting of that organization, reported as fact in the newspaper, and thus the myth was perpetuated.

According to this story, Anne Hill Carter Lee was said to be subject to mysterious fainting spells that produced a death-like state. After a prolonged illness in October of 1805, Anne Lee was pronounced dead by four physicians who were called to her bedside.

Her body was prepared for burial and placed in a coffin,

which was then placed on view in the Lee mansion for four days. At the end of that time, the coffin was then taken to the family mausoleum where a steady stream of visitors came to view the body. Seven days after Mrs. Lee's entombment, a servant came to the mausoleum to sweep up debris and litter that had accumulated after a procession of friends had viewed the "corpse" in its coffin for the last time. Hearing sounds emanating from the coffin, the servant gathered up enough nerve to raise the lid of the coffin. Inside, he saw Mrs. Lee's lips quivering and her eyelids fluttering. Though very frightened, the man hurried to the house for help. Mrs. Lee was taken to the manor house where she recovered. Fifteen months later, on January 19, 1807, Anne Carter Lee gave birth to a son she named Robert Edward Lee.

Serious historians, such as Douglas Southall Freeman, who is considered the official biographer of Robert E. Lee, refuted the allegation of the premature burial of Mrs. Lee.

Indeed, the curators and officials at Stratford Hall have always maintained that the story was not true. Their opinions are based primarily on the belief that if anything of this magnitude had truly occurred, then some mention of it would have been recorded in family documents such as diaries, journals, letters, and other family papers. Surely, Robert E. Lee himself would have mentioned in his recollections of his boyhood if such an event had taken place.

Myths such as these, by virtue of being retold countless times by people whose integrity is unquestioned, eventually become assimilated into the lore surrounding a notable figure and are thus accepted as fact. Repeated retelling lends an air of authenticity to the story, especially when attributed to people who claimed to have inside knowledge of such things. The story of Robert E. Lee's birth after the so-called "death" of his mother is without doubt a myth. Colin Lindsay's story, as regards his birth, may be fiction as well, but no one has ever stepped up to refute it.

Polly Wants a Drink

The Scots-Irish ancestry of many North Carolinians is most evident in the tales they spin. The most notable thing about these tales however, is that often they are true rather than fabricated in a whiskey-induced fog. Truth is stranger than fiction, and this is borne out in the following story told to me by a friend named Sandy. The story takes place in the early 1940s, and is so blatantly absurd that it has to be true.

Sandy's father, whom I will call N., as I was cautioned not to use real names, owned a grocery store on the outskirts of Laurinburg. During the Depression, N. was in the habit of allowing many of his customers who were strapped for cash to run a tab on their groceries. One such customer was an elderly lady who drove around in an automobile that was equipped with a perch on the dashboard for her pet parrot, Polly.

Now, this lady was well educated, and this fact had influenced Polly to the extent that the parrot had a decent vocabulary and was quite well behaved, though often very talkative. The lady repeatedly thanked N. for his generosity in extending credit to her, and she assured N. that she would remember him in her will.

Well, the day came when the old lady went on to her reward. In the course of time, when all of her affairs were settled, N. was surprised one day when the old lady's attorney appeared at the grocery store. He informed N. that this lady had named N. in her will as a beneficiary. She had left her automobile to him. The attorney also mentioned that Polly came with the car, cage and all.

After the initial shock wore off, N. began to feel that maybe it would be rather nice to be the owner of a parrot, so he had the cage installed at the automobile dealership he owned. N. felt that Polly would attract customers. What he failed to grasp, however, was that Polly was a fast learner, and N.'s friends were not only fond of whiskey, but were also the proud possessors of a vocabulary not suited for the average customer's ears. They spoke quite freely and explicitly around the parrot, so it was not surprising that Polly, whose I.Q, just possibly exceeded that of the characters who frequented the business, began to acquire a much more extensive vocabulary. In fact, N.'s wife complained that the parrot had the filthiest mouth she had ever heard. While the parrot's education was advancing, Polly also developed a propensity for the taste of whiskey, and when drunk, she would regale N.'s more disreputable cronies with a torrent of vulgarities and profanities. Polly would eventually pass out, lying on her back with her feet in the air.

As her fame spread, Polly became a sought after guest at some of their drinking parities. Sometimes she was lent out to enliven a party. Neighbors began complaining about the bird's foul language. Finally, one of the nearby neighbors had enough of the parrot's drunken behavior and comments on one such a night, and called the city police. When the police arrived, they took Polly into custody and incarcerated the parrot at the police station.

N. went down to the police station to bail out his errant parrot. The police, however, refused to release Polly until several days later when the bird was finally sober and had quieted down. N. took Polly back to the car dealership on a permanent basis. There Polly spent the rest of her days until that fateful day when she fell off the wagon, so to speak. Someone had sneaked Polly some whiskey, and had forgotten to close the cage door.

As Polly lay on her back, sleeping off the booze from the

night before, some rather large rats that were in the building got into the cage and made short work of poor Polly. Thus, the notorious Polly ended her days, eaten by rats while she lay in a drunken stupor on the floor of her cage. What an ignominious end to such a colorful life!

The Beast of Bladenboro
and Other Strange Happenings

Hoaxes have been perpetuated since the beginnings of civilization. Scotland County experienced its own homegrown hoax in the late 1930s. A local farmer went out to one of his fields one morning and was surprised to see gigantic footprints marching across the newly plowed field. In the days to come, others in the area were also treated to the appearance of huge footprints of something or someone that had walked across recently plowed fields. I was told that the mystery was eventually solved when local pranksters admitted to creating giant feet and using them to "walk" across the plowed fields. However, in light of the popularity of recent television programs about the elusive Sasquatch and the preponderance of evidence being released regarding these cryptids, perhaps the Scotland County tracks were not a hoax, but the ones who might shed some light on this tale are no longer around to substantiate the story. Was this story fact or fake? We'll probably never know.

Another more perplexing phenomenon with no satisfactory explanation occurred in January of 1954 in a small textile town in Bladen County, just about fifty miles east of Laurinburg. This series of events earned it the designation, "Beast of Bladenboro." The first story appeared in the *Charlotte Observer* and told of a woman who was hanging clothes on the line to dry when a large black animal streaked past her, heading for a swampy area. Other stories followed, all with various

50

accounts of personal encounters with a strange animal that was terrorizing the community. The first known victim was a goat that was found dead by its owner. According to local accounts, it had been drained of most of its blood.

One man told of being in his house one evening when he heard his dog howling as if in pain. He went out to see what was wrong and discovered his dog lying near the back of his property, badly torn and bleeding. He carried the dog back to the house and placed the dog on the porch while he went inside to get some supplies with which to treat the dog's wounds. Another screaming howl brought him rushing back to the porch, only to discover that his dog had been dragged off the porch by something that left a few tracks leading to the nearby swamp. According to his account, the dog had been drained of its blood. As the sightings and incidents grew, so did the hysteria.

Other people began to tell of their experiences with the mysterious beast. Many such stories involved finding bloodless chickens, cats, dogs, and other animals that had encountered the beast. There were tales of hunters with tracking dogs following a trail only to discover at some point that whatever they had been tracking was actually stalking them. The stories appeared with more frequency in the newspapers, and yet, no one was able to capture the creature. Eventually the sightings stopped altogether in the little town of Bladenboro, although there were a few isolated reports from the surrounding area for a while. Things quieted down, but no explanations were ever offered for the series of events that happened there. Someone did offer the possibility of an escaped panther from a traveling circus, but there was little upon which to base that theory.

Recently, I came across an article in a local newspaper that mentioned the fact that the town of Bladenboro needed to find some way of bringing more money into the area. As tourism is a popular solution for economic growth these days, the town of Bladenboro decided to come up with a plan to increase tourism

51

to this community. They needed a logo, and came up with the idea of using the "Beast" on their logo. The "Beast" has been affectionately and officially named "BOB," an acronym for – you guessed it – "Beast of Bladenboro."

The year 1954, when the beast was ravishing Bladenboro, was the same year that Hurricane Hazel laid waste to the North and South Carolina coasts with an eighteen-foot storm surge that inundated Ocean Isle in North Carolina and created intensive damage inland for more than one hundred miles. It was also the year that my brother Billy enlivened the Presbyterian Christmas Eve service by making a rather irreverent remark during the choir's performance that sent those gathered there into paroxysms of suppressed laughter and giggles.

A Great Bald Eagle

The church choir director was Oscar Blue McCormick, an old (at least he was to us, anyway) baldheaded bachelor who was quite portly as well as being short of stature. Because that particular evening service was primarily a musical one, all of the various choirs had been massed in the chancel of the church. A small low table had been placed in the center aisle of the church for Oscar Blue, as we called him, to stand upon so that he could direct all of the choirs and so that they would be able to see him as well. As the service began, Oscar Blue, dressed in a full dark-colored choir robe, stepped up on the table and raised his arms to get the attention of the choirs. The collar of the choir robe bunched up around his neck, which pushed up and revealed several thick folds of skin as he raised his bald head to commence the Christmas musical program.

It was at that moment that my happy-go-lucky brother observed in a loud stage whisper heard by most of those around us, "He looks like a great bald eagle ready to take off." Of course, I had to giggle, as did several of our friends sitting beside us. My mother, on the other side of Billy, nudged him rather sharply with her elbow. By then, we were all trying, without much success, to keep from giggling aloud.

In the meantime, Oscar Blue was on the table, vigorously directing the choirs with elaborate hand, arm, and body motions, the loose sleeves of his choir robe flapping. My mother's shoulders began shaking in an effort to suppress her own laughter. Soon others sitting in our pew, as well as the pews in front and behind, also began choking back their own

53

laughter, many with tears rolling down their faces. The more people tried to control themselves, the worse the situation got.

Throughout the entire service, Billy was sitting there looking straight ahead, a small angelic smirk tugging at the corners of his mouth. None of the rest us could look at him. With the exception of those seated near us, no one was really quite certain why he or she was laughing, but laughter is contagious, particularly when it occurs in places generally considered inappropriate.

Somehow, the program continued, and finally reached a successful conclusion, and a number of greatly relieved church members filed out of the church rather quickly, still wearing idiotic grins on their faces. The instigator of the whole mess innocently strolled out with the rest of the churchgoers, his "angelic" face alight with the pleasure he had contributed to the concert. For many, it was truly a night to remember.

Way Down Upon the Lumbee River

During the time I was growing up, there were three separate school systems: white, black, and Indian. The Indians in this area were known at that time by the appellate "Croatan" The name got its origin in the carving found on a tree on Roanoke Island when Governor John White returned from a trip to England and found the colony he had established on the island was gone without a trace. The only clue to its disappearance was the word, "CROATOAN" carved on a tree. In later years, many of the Indians that lived in our area were born with dark blonde hair and blue or green eyes. They were said to be descendants of that Lost Colony. Eventually, the Indians living in our area began to call themselves Lumbees. Today, the Lumbee tribe is the largest Native American tribe east of the Mississippi River. Only recently have the Lumbees been granted tribal status by the government. The tribe continues to strive toward full recognition by the federal government.

Perhaps the most infamous of the Lumbee inhabitants was one Henry Berry Lowry who would become a folk hero, akin in many respects to Jesse James. That legendary figure was a man who began leader of a band of outlaws that terrorized Robeson County in the latter years of the War Between the States and continuing well into the Reconstruction era.

In order to understand fully the impact this outlaw band had on Robeson County, it is necessary to first look at the family origins that gave rise to Henry Berry, as he was familiarly called by family and friends. According to most sources, in 1769 a man by the name of James Lowry and his half-breed Tuscarora wife moved from the mountains of Franklin County, North Carolina, to the swamplands of Robeson County. James and his wife had three sons, one of whom, William Lowry, fought in the American Revolution and suffered a severe wound from a saber cut. For his service to the American cause, he received a Federal pension. One of William's sons, Allen Lowry, married a woman of Portuguese descent named Pollie Cumba or Cumbo. The resulting large family from this union would include four sons, William, Steven, Thomas, and Henry Berry, who would write the Lowry name indelibly into Robeson County history.

While accounts of the incidents that led to the formation of the Lowry gang vary in detail according to the person recounting the events, including some that rely on so-called "official" records, the origins of the formation of the gang remain remarkably similar.

Many believe that the Lowry gang grew out of a dubious incident that occurred in 1864, when the Home Guard in Robeson County believed that some members of the Lowry family were harboring stolen goods from a series of burglaries in the area. In one version of the story, a neighbor had tried for years to get Allen Lowry to sell some of his property, which was a 300-acre land grant from King George in 1732. When he refused, the neighbor, a member of the Home Guard and his sons hatched a plot to hide stolen goods on the Lowry property. A posse of thirty men marched out to Lowry swamp to the home of Allen Lowry and searched it, turning up the stolen property. A court martial was held on the spot and Allen Lowry and one of his sons were found guilty and given a death sentence. The posse thought that the sentence should be executed immediately, and one conceived of the idea of having the two men dig their own graves. While Pollie and some of her children sat fearfully inside the Lowry cabin, Allen and his son dug the graves, and were then summarily executed on the spot.

Henry Berry Lowry then seventeen years of age, had been out hunting and was returning home with a brace of wild turkeys when he heard rifle shots. Stealthily creeping up to the cabin, he arrived just in time to witness the execution of his father and one of his brothers. When the posse left Lowry swamp, Henry Berry, still in hiding, meticulously counted the men as they passed by, and noted that there were thirty men.

After filling in the graves of his father and elder brother, Henry Berry Lowry, in a spirit of sworn revenge, vowed not to rest until the thirty men who participated in the deaths of his father and brother were dead. Forming a band of his brothers William, Steven, and Thomas, brothers-in-law Boss Strong and Andrew Strong, a white man, Zach T. McLaughlin, Henderson Oxendine, Calvin Oxendine, John Dial, George Applewhite, and himself as their leader, the gang terrorized Robeson County for perhaps ten years. The band drew support from all three races. If the legal system could not exact retribution for the willful murder of a man, then the responsibility for such retribution fell upon that man's kinsmen.

The Lowry band set up their headquarters near Pembroke in a loosely knit community called Scuffletown, or as some spell it, Scuffletoun. Their camp had a front and back entrance, a trap door, and a tunnel that led deep into an impenetrable swamp that was familiar territory to the band.

Henry Berry Lowry had been courting young sixteen-year-old Rhoda Strong, a sister of Boss Strong. On December 7, 1865, the two were married at a ceremony at the old Lowry homestead. Hector J. McLean, a white friend and a justice of the peace, performed the wedding ceremony. The festivities were hardly underway when a company of the Home Guard arrived at the Lowry homestead, and, charging Henry Berry with the murder of James P. Barnes took him prisoner.

Lowry was imprisoned in the Whiteville jail. According to Lumbee legends, Rhoda visited him in jail and slipped a file to him in a cake. Whatever the truth of that may be, it is fact that Lowrie managed to escape the jail by filing his way through the window bars.

In 1976, Randolph Umberger wrote an outdoor historical drama he titled *Strike at the Wind*. This drama recounts the Henry Berry Lowry story. With a cast and crew of sixty, this production has run every night from July through September in Pembroke, North Carolina, since 1976 until the 2004 season when there was no production due to lack of funding. After remaining closed for two years, during the summer of 2006, *Strike at the Wind* was revived, and apparently did rather well, attracting some 300 spectators each night. Hopefully this will be a permanent feature down in the land of the Lumbee.

A memorable incident occurred in January of 1958 that would change forever the cultural history of Scotland and Robeson counties. The Ku Klux Klan, while rather active in some areas, was not a viable force in Scotland County. A group of hooded Klansmen from neighboring South Carolina came into Robeson County to the little town of Maxton. Their goal was to curtail efforts to integrate the white and Indian schools, which, in at least some of the cases, had been somewhat integrated to begin with. They also thought to restore the Ku Klux Klan organization in Robeson County.

Descendants of Henry Berry Lowry attended the Klan rally in Maxton after a cross was burned in the yard of a Lumbee who had moved into a white neighborhood. Another was also ignited in front of the house of a white woman who was supposedly was having an affair with a Lumbee man.

The following account of the confrontation between the two groups was related to me by Sanford Locklear in March of 2006. Mr. Locklear was a man in his seventies who vividly told me his version of what ensued:

According to Mr. Locklear, he and his family and friends had learned that a radio preacher by the name of "Catfish" Cole was planning to bring the Ku Klux Klan from South Carolina to Lumberton for a Klan rally. Apparently, he had used his radio sermons to denounce interracial dating and socializing. His plans including burning several crosses in front of the homes of those engaging in such activities. The barbershop in Pembroke was a local gathering place for the men, and Cole's threat was the topic of conversation among the Lumbee patrons there. Sanford Locklear was a young man living nearby, and he and some cousins decided that it was just not right for the Klan to get involved in their personal affairs. They vowed to intervene and stop the Klan once and for all. The young men went to their respective homes and told others what they planned to do. It was not long before a large contingent of Indians gathered and met at a bridge near Maxton, a bridge that the Klan members would have to cross as they marched on to Pembroke and to Lumberton where they planned to stage a large rally.

Locklear and his friends were waiting when the cars carrying Klansmen from South Carolina began to arrive at the bridge. Some of the Lumbees were armed with shotguns in case they ran into trouble. They surrounded "Catfish" Cole, and someone shot out a light bulb on a nearby utility pole. During the melee that followed, the Klan members were forced off the bridge, and many of them began running away in all directions, leaving their parked cars behind. The ringleader, "Catfish" Cole ran also. Locklear speculates that some members of the Klan who had not yet reached the site most likely picked up those who chose to run. The Lumbees, hardly intimidated by the white-sheeted Klan, donned feathered headdresses, armed themselves with tomahawks, and quite literally chased the Klan out of the area, to the great chagrin of the Klan. The media had a field day reporting the event, and national coverage brought the action right into our homes via television.

In the January 27, 1958, issue of *Newsweek Magazine,* an account of what occurred differed somewhat from the account told by Mr. Locklear. That story stated that the Indians let the Klan set up a microphone and a single electric light bulb in the rallying area.

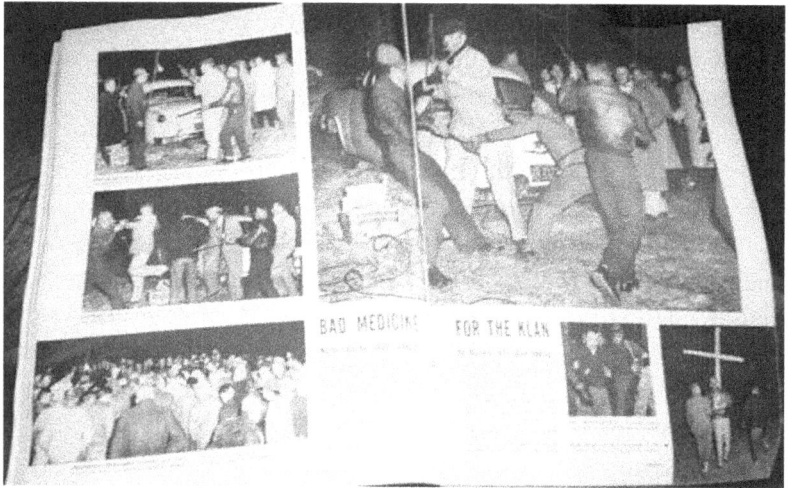

The January 27, 1958, issue of *Newsweek Magazine*

Approximately one hundred Klansmen assembled around a truck, which soon was surrounded by Indians who called for the Klan Wizard, the Rev. James W. "Catfish" Cole, to show himself. Cole, however, stayed behind the truck. Some of the Indians fired guns in the air, and one shot out the single light bulb. The Klansmen, who were well armed, threw down weapons and ran for their cars and trucks. Deputies from the Robeson County Sheriff's Department fired tear-gas bombs into the melee. When the air cleared, the Lumbee raid was over. It was the shortest Ku Klux Klan rally in history. It was also the end of plans for establishing the Klan in that neck of the woods.

On August 22, 2006, Sanford Locklear, age 72, died at his home after an extensive illness. A lifelong member and an ordained deacon of Rock of Ages Baptist Church in Red Springs, Locklear was involved in many community affairs. He was a longtime member of the Lumbee Tribal Council and represented that group in various capacities.

He, too, had his moment of fame and his day in the sun.

Sanford Locklear

The Lost Child Israel

In the early part of the 1950s, I was the proud owner of a Tennessee walking horse named Lady. Several children and adults in our neighborhood owned horses as well. Often on weekends, the adults and tag-along-children with mounts would go riding as a group. On a few occasions, we would ride to a small restaurant on the outskirts of town and eat supper before returning home. It was always an event I looked forward to.

On other occasions, however, I would get up on a Saturday morning, saddle my horse, and go for a ride. I never went too far from home, but always rode to the old sandpit not far from my house. One day, I took a different route and rode across a broom sedge field into a clump of old oak trees growing on a slight rise. The site was probably no more than a mile from our house. I had never been in that spot before, so I was surprised to find a number of tombstones scattered among the trees. Most of the ones I could see bore dates in the late 1800s. I was quite excited by my discovery, as no one had ever mentioned there was a cemetery that close to our house. When I questioned my mother about the cemetery, she was unaware that it was there.

On my next visit, I brought a small notebook and a pencil, and set about copying the information written on the stones. I am not sure how many stones I found, but I imagine there were at least ten or twelve. When I returned home after my foray to this cemetery, I got out an old portable typewriter and set about typing up a list of the graves and their inscriptions. One of the surnames that kept cropping up in my list was the name

"Israel" or "Esrael." No one by that name had ever lived in the area, as far as I could determine from questioning several people. Eventually, I gave up trying to solve that mystery, and soon forgot about the cemetery as other interests became more important.

Some fifteen years later, I was teaching in Fernandina Beach, Florida, and was talking to one of my co-workers who was originally from West Virginia. In the course of our conversation, she told me a story of a group of people who left West Virginia and traveled by rafts or flatboats down rivers into the southern part of North Carolina. Somewhere on this arduous journey, the people fell sick and died along the way. The only one to survive was a very young boy, perhaps still in infancy, who drifted on the raft until it was spotted by some settlers. The child was rescued, but because of his age was not able to tell them who he was. The kind-hearted people who took him in gave him the name "Israel." Their rationale in choosing his name reflected upon their familiarity with the Old Testament in the Bible, which spoke of the lost tribe of Israel. My co-worker told me that when the child named Israel was grown and married, the name "Israel" was used as his surname.

Although, there was no way of connecting that story with those of the Israel's I had discovered in that small cemetery, it was slightly disconcerting to say the least.

In the meantime, a local man and former mayor, with an interest in the history of Scotland, made a more intense inventory of the small burial ground. Along with other small cemeteries in the county, he published a book that was placed in the local public library. When I finally returned to Laurinburg for a visit, I located the list I had typed so many years before and gave a copy to the library. The list was inserted in the book of cemeteries compiled by the former mayor. A comparison of his list and mine showed that I had listed some that he had missed. Unfortunately, the last time I checked, the list had been removed from the book, and the copy I kept no longer exists.

As time passed, Winn-Dixie Stores purchased the property with the idea of building a grocery store. The location was a good one, because a bypass went nearly in front of the property, and the city of Laurinburg was expanding in that direction. A company that specializes in moving cemeteries surveyed the property and arranged for moving the graves to another location.

Because the local newspaper, *The Laurinburg Exchange,* did a story on the cemetery, I learned that it was believed that the Israel or Esrael family was a family of Syrians who lived here in the county in the late 1800s. Evidently, many of them died, perhaps due to an influenza epidemic. The Gibson family, who owned the property near where the Syrians lived, permitted them to bury their dead there. The Gibsons had already had some family members buried there.

Whether these so-called "Syrians" had any connection with the West Virginia pilgrims and the lost child that was taken in by strangers is only a matter of conjecture. Sheer coincidences do occur, but the story told to me did invoke some eerie feelings when it was related to me. The area where the graveyard was located was part of a large tract of farmland at one time, but by the 1950s had been split up and divided by several people. Some of it was still being farmed when I was growing up, but much of it was left uncultivated and had been taken over by Scotch broom sedge. Had I found remnants of the relatives of the lost child, Israel? It would be interesting to learn more about who these people were and how they got to Scotland County. The graveyard is gone now, as are the graves. Although the remains were reburied in a private cemetery, the memory of these people has been erased and forgotten. Were they just "poor way-faring strangers" who were passing through? Occasionally, the name does crop up, but it is certainly not common in the area.

Those Red Clay Hills of Georgia

My grandfather, William Joseph Green was born in Paulding County, Georgia, in 1868. He married Fannie Rockmore, daughter of J. P. Rockmore, a large landowner in Walton County, about 1890. They had two children, Guy, born 1892, and Joseph, born in 1894. At that time, they were living in Covington, Georgia. Fannie died in 1894, shortly after the birth of Joseph. Will Green was left with two very young children to rear, and since the youngest was just an infant, it was imperative that he find a new wife as soon as possible

I do not know how Will met Era Watson, but their courtship was obviously a brief one because one Sunday in 1894, the two went for a buggy ride, found a Justice of the Peace, and came back to Loganville married.

Era's father was Francis Moten Watson, a Confederate veteran who came from Gwinnett County to Walton County after "The War," planted a small allowance of cotton and other small crops, and carried the mail on the Stone Mountain postal route.

Francis Moten Watson, CSA

He married Elizabeth Frances Nix, daughter of Harrison and Catherine Ford Nix, in 1870, and together they had five daughters, Era, Mary, Ellen, Belinda, and Lilla.

Era Watson Green settled rather happily in her new home

with her new husband and two very young little stepsons, Guy and Joe. As the two little boys matured, they developed the usual sibling rivalry, and fought between themselves over the things little boys everywhere fight over. They disrupted my grandmother's tranquil life until one day she called them to her side and had a serious chat with them about their unruly behavior. She concluded her lecture with the warning: "If you boys do not stop misbehaving and fighting with each other, the Devil is going to come after you!"

Well, now every child of that day and time knew exactly what the Devil looked like.

He was a tall man with horns and a tail, and he carried chains with him to capture unwary, sinful souls. This idea was sufficient to curb the boys' fighting for a time. However, late one afternoon the two were playing in the woods near their house. One thing led to another, and soon they began fighting in earnest. Suddenly, they heard a noise in the woods, and ceased fighting long enough to hear the clank, clank, clank, of dragging chains. Horrified, they both began running for home as fast as they could. They dashed inside the house and threw themselves in Era's lap.

"The Devil is coming after us! We could hear his chains. He's coming! He's coming to get us!" they sobbed hysterically, faces pale and frightened.

Era gathered them into her arms and held them tightly, assuring them that she would do her best not to let the Devil get them. However, she reminded them that they needed to mend their ways, that their constant fighting with each other was not an acceptable pastime. The boys solemnly promised that they would certainly not engage in any more fighting with each other. This time, they kept their promise. It was only after they were grown that Era told the story of how Robert, a Negro farmer who owned some property on the other side of the woods, had been plowing his fields with a mule that day. As it was getting late in the day, he unhitched the mule, gave it a

66

slap, and sent it home, the traces and chains of the plow and harness dragging behind it and clanking every step of the way. This random act forever altered the two little boys' relationship with each other. They never forgot that the Devil himself had once threatened their little world.

In 1900, Era and Will's first child was born, a son they named Herman Alto Green. Three years later my mother, Lottie Elizabeth, was born. Jack, Ethel, and Walter soon followed. The family of seven children and two adults lived first in Gwinnett County, and then moved to Loganville in the adjoining Walton County. Ethel, born in 1906, only lived three months. Herman died in 1918 of diphtheria. Lottie graduated from high school in 1918 and went to college at Georgia Normal and Industrial Institute in Milledgeville, earning a Bachelor's degree in 1922, the only member of her family to earn a college degree. Her brothers later moved to Atlanta where they eventually married, established businesses, and had families.

The Sight and Other Interesting Tidbits

My mother always insisted that her mother, Era Watson Green, was a rather skeptical person who was seldom given to relating things that smacked of the occult or the supernatural. Nevertheless, Era was of Scottish descent, and though she did not advertise it, she possessed what modern would-be psychics refer to as extrasensory perception, but what the old Scots called "the sight"; that is, the ability to see into the future or to make predictions. Although, I never knew my maternal grandmother, as she died in 1934, four years before I was born, my mother did tell of two incidents she recalled her mother relating in a rare revealing moment.

Some wild horses were once brought into Loganville and penned up in a small corral near the railroad tracks. They were to be loaded onto a railway car for shipment to another place. They had never been broken, and the men had difficulty getting them all into the enclosure where they would stay overnight. Late that afternoon, my grandmother saw the horses running around the enclosure, kicking and bucking. Then, to her amazement, the horses suddenly calmed down, and she saw a man wearing a white shirt with the sleeves rolled up, strolling through the horse corral, petting and soothing the horses. He seemed to have no fear of them at all. She stepped off the porch of her house and walked toward the corral to see who this strange man was. She clearly saw him standing in the middle of the herd. As she came closer, however, he vanished. When she later told the owners of the horses what she observed, they denied knowing or seeing anyone who fit the description she gave and they had not sent any of their own workers into the corral with the horses.

The other incident was one my own mother witnessed many times when she was growing up. The phenomenon centered on the old rambling house where she grew up. The house was one of those large old country houses, with heart pine floors and walls. A large porch extended across the front and boasted a swing suspended from the ceiling. The old kitchen at the rear of the house opened onto a partially enclosed porch that was built around a deep well. On the other side of the porch was another room, originally a bedroom. The house had belonged to my great-grandparents. It was built prior to the War Between the States. It had a chimney made of river stones and a tin roof.

My mother remembered sitting with the rest of the family in the parlor of the house one evening when a door that led from the parlor to an unused bedroom slowly opened in full view of everyone sitting there. My grandmother calmly got up and closed the door firmly, engaging the small metal latch on the doorframe. In a few minutes, they all watched the latch slowly disengage from its hook, and the door once more swing open. My mother told how my grandmother quietly spoke and said, "He means no harm. He just misses human company." This incident was repeated on numerous occasions, and then gradually ceased. No explanation was ever offered as to the cause of this phenomenon, nor was the entity ever identified.

Other stories relating to this small town in Walton County concerned mostly family members. As with many Southern families, there was always at least one relative who exhibited traits that others in the family felt were better kept hidden from polite society as much as possible, although tales of their foibles frequently cropped up in family conversations. Nearly every family had its skeleton in the proverbial closet. In my mother's family there was Uncle Ves Cox who was a little too fond of spirits, the bottled kind, that is. My mother often related the time Uncle Ves, who had been out celebrating some obscure occasion with his male cohorts, came home in an inebriated state, and in an attempt to cross a log over the small creek back of their house, lost his footing and fell, straddling the log. The family awakened to the loud shouts of "Giddy up! Giddy Up, you *%!& *# mule!" Upon investigating the source of these exhortations, my great-grandfather Watson found Uncle Ves, astride the log, whipping it with a stick, and yelling at the top of his lungs to what he had perceived to be an obstinate mule.

Christmas in Loganville held especially dear memories to my mother. She told us how her father and mother would put up the Christmas tree in the parlor on Christmas Eve. The children never saw the tree until Christmas morning. The tree would remain in the parlor until Kings' Day or Epiphany on January 6th. After breakfast, the parlor doors were opened, the Christmas tree in all its glory was finally revealed, and presents were then exchanged. My grandfather would then concoct a very large punchbowl of eggnog for his male friends who would drop in for a sip later in the day. My mother recounted how some of the young men in the little town would dress up in outlandish, feminine costumes and ride their horses through the town, singing and shouting, and stopping at various houses to wish the occupants a Merry Christmas and accept a cup of eggnog. The young men called themselves "The Fantastics" and their practice, "Riding the Fantastic." I am not sure of the origin of this custom, but I have come across a few references to it from time to time.

I visited Loganville many times when I was about nine or ten years old. By that time, my great-aunt Mary, a spinster or more commonly called, an old maid, and Hilda, my first cousin once removed, and her husband occupied the old house. They did not have indoor plumbing when I first went to visit there. That situation was finally remedied a few years after my cousin married and the newly-weds wanted some of the modern conveniences. The back porch was built around a stone well, and the house itself was constructed almost entirely of heart pine. I always enjoyed staying with them for a few days in the summer time because I could sleep on a featherbed, play in the small creek that crossed the back of their property, play with the numerous kittens that were always present, and explore underneath the house which was supported by stone pillars in the back. I used to love the rainy nights when I could lie in bed and listen to the rain hitting the old tin roof.

The old house was sold in the late 1950s to a man who had it moved to another location. I do not know if the new owners had any unusual experiences to occur in the house. My cousin and her husband built a new, modern house on the property after the death of my great-aunt. Once when my husband and I stopped by Loganville to see my cousin, her husband, Ed, took us for a drive and showed me the old house in its new location. Somehow, things had changed and there was no longer a sense of familiarity with the house. It had been robbed of its distinctive personality that I remembered from my childhood. On the other hand, perhaps, I had just grown too far away from it in time and in distance.

Lottie Greene taught school for a year in Roswell, Georgia, but then moved back home with her parents who had by this time moved to Atlanta to a house out on Howell Mill Road. It was while she was working in the office of the Great Atlantic and Pacific Tea Company, that she met Albert Bernard Carpenter who was working as an accountant for the company. They fell in love and were married in Atlanta in 1925. Will Green referred to Bernie as "that damn Yankee son-in- law who was born in Minnesota." When Will had occasion to be really angry with my father, he just called him "that goddamn Yankee." Through it all, my father kept his temper and soon made peace with Will Green. In 1926, their first child, Albert Bernard Carpenter, Jr., was born in Atlanta. They called him "Skippy." In 1929, they moved to Wilmington, North Carolina.

Cape Fear

My mother was always fascinated by history and legends, and it was during her time in Wilmington, that my mother first heard stories of old Wilmington, which she would later tell to us when my brother and I pestered her to "Tell us a story." The following are those I remember most vividly. They became a part of our family lore.

Oakdale Cemetery, located at the corner of Fifteenth and Market streets, was chartered in 1852. It covers about 165 acres and is the final resting place for many famous and prominent people. My paternal grandfather and grandmother are buried there. A huge number of yellow fever victims are buried there as well. Its winding paths, gigantic oaks and magnolias, and hanging moss provide a fitting backdrop for the stories my mother told.

One of the first stories about Oakdale that I remember hearing from her was the story of Nancy Martin, the daughter of a Wilmington merchant, who accompanied her father, Silas Martin, and brother, John, on a lengthy sea voyage. While at sea, Nancy became very ill and died. Mr. Martin did not wish to bury his daughter at sea, as was usually the custom. Turning back to Wilmington was not an option, since he had business contracts he felt obligated to honor.

The solution to this dilemma involved seating the body in a chair and placing it into a huge cask, which was then filled with rum and sealed. The grieving Silas Martin then continued his voyage. Misfortune seemed to follow Mr. Martin, however. His son John was apparently washed overboard during a storm.

His disappearance was not discovered until the next morning. The ship turned back and searched miles of sea, with the hope that at least his body could be recovered. When this search proved fruitless, Martin decided to return to Wilmington to tell his wife of the tragedy and also to bury his daughter. The cask of rum, containing Nancy's body, was buried intact at Oakdale Cemetery, and a small rugged cross with the name "Nance" placed on the grave. On the large family monument is an inscription for John Slater Martin, which reads. "Lost At Sea, September, 1857."

One of the most poignant stories my mother told about Oakdale, which was sure to produce tears in our eyes, was that of Captain William Ellerbrook, who was master of a tugboat on the Cape Fear River. The story begins on a night in February of 1880 when a fire broke out in a large store near the waterfront. In those days firemen relied on volunteers to help in fighting fires. Capt. Ellerbrook saw the fire and hurried from his boat that was docked nearby to help save some of the merchandise in the store from the flames. His dog followed him. Ellerbrook asked a bystander to hold his dog while he joined those trying to fight the fire. The fire became larger, and suddenly a loud scream came from the burning building. The dog, recognizing his master's voice, pulled loose from the bystander holding him and ran into the burning building.

When the ashes had cooled enough to allow firemen into the remains of the building the next day, they found the body of Capt. Ellerbrook lying face down beneath a fallen beam. Next to him was the body of his faithful dog, Boss, gripping a portion of Ellerbrook's coat in his teeth, where he had tried to pull his master to safety. The funeral was held the next day, and community leaders had decided that it was only fitting that the dog should lie in the arms of the master he loved so well. The two were buried together in the same casket. A monument erected by the city shows an inscription for Captain Ellerbrook on one face. On the opposite face of the stone is carved the figure of a sleeping dog in relief with the inscription, "Faithful Unto Death."

The other stories involving Oakdale included the story of Rose O'Neal Greenhow, the daring Confederate spy who drowned near Fort Fisher at the mouth of the Cape Fear River trying to swim ashore after her boat overturned. Gold she had sewn into her clothing weighted her down. When her body was recovered from the rocks, she was accorded a public military hero's funeral and buried with a Confederate flag covering her coffin. I did not know of many heroines at that time of my life, but Rose was definitely at the top of my short list, followed by Joan of Arc, Flora McDonald, and Nancy Drew. I used to pretend that I was swimming the dangerous river currents to carry messages to the Rebel troops. Other stories included that of an elderly woman who had been confined to her bed for many years. When she died, she was buried, bed and all, at Oakdale Cemetery.

Another story told of a woman whose husband died and was placed inside the family mausoleum. On one of her visits to place flowers inside the mausoleum, the heavy door closed and locked with her inside. In vain, she screamed and pounded on the door, but there was no one to hear her. She was discovered lying on the floor of the mausoleum by a caretaker sometime the next day. Her hair had turned completely white overnight. Her fingernails were broken and bloody from trying to claw her way out. She had died of the frightening experience of being locked overnight in the tomb.

Orton Plantation, a few miles south of Wilmington, on the Cape Fear River, also figured in many of the stories, as did other plantations along the river road. Orton's family graveyard, with its ghostly Spanish moss-draped trees, told the sad stories of lives cut short in the wake of yellow fever and other fevers that were prevalent in the low country. Our own feelings about mortality changed as we realized that children could and did die young, a rather novel idea to us, who were certain we would live forever.

One of these old plantation sites along the river was the family home of twin brothers. As young men, they were fond of hunting, racing, and other pursuits indulged in by the gentry at that period of time. During one of their hunting trips, one of the brother's was thrown from his horse. A doctor was summoned who pronounced the young man dead. His body was taken back to his house, placed in a coffin, and after proper ceremonies, was accordingly buried in the family graveyard.

His surviving twin was profoundly upset over the death of his brother. His sleep was disturbed by dreams in which his twin spoke to him, asking repeatedly, "Why did you let them bury me?"

The young man could stand it no longer. He took some friends with him to the burial place, and dug up his brother's grave. When the coffin was lifted from the ground, and the lid removed, the body of his brother was discovered lying face down in the coffin. His hands were bloodied, and the coffin lining shredded. The young man had regained consciousness, and had tried to claw his way out of his coffin. The distraught twin sadly reburied his brother who had been buried alive. Tales such as this were common in the 1800s when medical knowledge was oftentimes sketchy, and it was not that unusual for someone to be prematurely declared dead. The days of brain scans and other devices were more than a hundred years up the road, and doctors had to rely primarily on what they could observe at first hand, based on knowledge acquired as they practiced.

We also were told that there were tunnels in Wilmington, and these had been used by jailhouse escapees, runaway slaves, and others engaged in nefarious affairs. It was somewhat devastating when I later learned that the so-called "tunnels" were in actuality little more than storm drains. In fact, one of the tunnels was created when Jacob's Run, a stream that used to run through downtown Wilmington, was actually covered over, and the street was then paved over the route of the old streambed.

And Then the Yankees Came

My grandmother Carpenter, my father's mother, was born in 1881 on a farm in Minnesota. Her father, Henry Hammond Williamson, was a cooper by profession, but tried his hand at some farming on the side. Her mother, Mary Eliza Holmes, was Virginia born and bred.

Her childhood was very different from that of my Southern kin, and we were always fascinated with her stories of blizzards and tornadoes, or cyclones as she called them. The farm had a cyclone cellar where the family took refuge during the severe electrical storms that were prevalent in that part of the country. It must have been frightening to a young girl to be awakened by her parents in the middle of the night and bustled out to the cyclone cellar to ride out a storm, but that was life on a Midwestern farm.

She once told us of going to a party with a group of young people during the winter. They traveled to the party in a horse-drawn sleigh, as there had been a particularly heavy snowstorm the day before. That night however, the sky was clear and a bright moon shone down on the snow. The route back home took them through some deep woods. As they were riding along, the horse began to show signs of nervousness, and one person in the group noticed some shadowy forms following the sleigh. My grandmother's brother who was driving the horse urged it to go faster and yet the pursuing creatures managed to keep up. Eventually they came to a clearing, and there in the light cast by the moon, they saw a pack of wolverines running along the edge of the woods. Arriving finally, and safely, home they learned that a neighbor had encountered the pack of wolverines near his home, and had actually been attacked by them. He managed to drive them off and escaped without serious harm.

My grandfather Carpenter was born in 1879 in Essex County, in upstate New York. His parents, Alvina Carpenter and William Frederick Bailey, married very young, very much against their parents' wishes. Their first child, Albert Hiram Bailey was born in 1876 in AuSable Forks. A second child, William Frederick Bailey was born in 1879. Sadly, Alvina did not survive the second childbirth. The baby died a day or two later. Both mother and child were buried together in the windswept cemetery in Upper Jay with the Adirondack Mountains as a backdrop.

Evidently, some ill feelings over Alvina's death were very much in evidence, for her father blamed William for causing her death. Apparently, harsh words were exchanged, for the records of the Methodist Episcopal Church in AuSable Forks state that Bernard Carpenter, father of Alvina Carpenter Bailey, was removed from the church rolls for "profane swearing." Bernard took young Albert into his home, and because there were only girls in the Carpenter household, "adopted" Albert and gave him the Carpenter name. Whether this was a legal formal adoption or merely an adoption by virtue of the act is not clear, but the child henceforth was known as Albert Hiram Carpenter. His father, William Bailey, eventually remarried and left New York. He ended up in California where he worked with the Sheriff's Department in Santa Monica.

In 1881, the Carpenter family left AuSable Forks and moved to St. Paul, Minnesota. It was in this region that my grandfather grew up. My grandfather would be a grown man with grandchildren before he learned that his birth father was living in Rutland, Vermont. They corresponded with each other, but never met face to face. William Bailey finally moved to Santa Monica, and it was there he died at the age of 83.

Bert, as my grandfather was called, led an interesting, if somewhat varied life. As a young man, he worked in the stockyards around Brighton, Minnesota. He was once hired to break, train, and drive a mule train carrying dynamite to the newly discovered gold fields in the Yukon Territory. One of his letters mentions that his route took him through the famed White Horse Pass.

His life's calling however, led him to the field of veterinary medicine, a field still very much in the fledgling stages at that time. Most veterinarians learned by working with other "horse doctors," and I have no reason to suppose that my grandfather was an exception to this common practice. He had a horse that he showed at county fairs, and also raised chickens of various breeds, one of which, a Buff Orphington, won a trophy at one of the fairs.

My grandfather took a job with the U. S. Department of Agriculture as a veterinarian. This position was primarily involved in meat inspections and necessitated the family's moving all over the county. They lived in Ohio, Pennsylvania, New York, New Jersey, Georgia, and finally in Wilmington, North Carolina. It was in Wilmington that my grandfather was assigned to the U. S. Customs House. It was there he died in 1937 of a heart attack while driving their maid home.

Down to the Sea

My own encounter with things unexplained occurred when I was sixteen. I had been asleep in my room when I suddenly awakened to see the gray figure of an elderly man wearing an old-fashioned suit and a wide brim hat. The figure appeared to glide across the room and then stopped near the foot of the bed. I sat up in bed, grabbed my pillow and threw it at the figure. At the same time, I switched on the lamp beside my bed. There was no one there!

I sat there shaking and breathing rather rapidly, trying to convince myself that I had had a bad dream. I was not successful. My pillow lay on the floor near the foot of the bed where I had thrown it at the intruder. I later told my mother what I had seen. Surprisingly enough, she did not brush it off with the expected comment that I had been dreaming. She did tell me that when our house was built, the foundations of a chimney and other brickwork had been uncovered in the front yard. She made no attempt to offer an explanation of what I had seen. Several days later, while in the back yard kicking some dirt around with my foot, I uncovered a dark reddish-brown cameo. I still have it, and I suppose that it may support my mother's notion that an earlier dwelling occupied the land where our house stands. Certainly no one in the family recognized it as belonging to anyone they knew. It was obviously old and had been buried for quite a while.

More than fifteen years later, I was to witness other strange happenings for which there were no satisfactory explanations. At that time, I had graduated from the University at Chapel Hill, and had accepted a teaching position in Fernandina Beach, Florida.

Fernandina Beach, Florida, in 1961, was still a small fishing village located on the western portion of Amelia Island, one of the so-called Golden Isles that dot both the Georgia coast and the coast of northern Florida as well. Its early history was a roll call of French, Spanish, Indian, Portuguese, and English names, and it had had eight different flags flown over it at various periods. The island was bounded on the west by the St. Mary's River and on the east by the Atlantic Ocean. The old town, site of an early Spanish fort, was located about a mile northwest of the present town site. Fort Clinch was near the northern end of the island. Amelia Island's main industries were the pulp mill and shrimping. A lighthouse in the central part of the island completed the picture of a quaint little island. Legends of pirates and their hidden treasures abounded. It had, after all, a long history as a seafaring village.

I was a brand new college graduate of the University of North Carolina in Chapel Hill, all set to conquer the world, and I had just signed a contract to teach in the junior high school in Fernandina. I was excited about all the prospects ahead, never dreaming that Fernandina would change my life forever. But such are the vagaries of life.

It was there, on that sandy little Amelia Island, that I met the man who would later become my husband. John was born in Savannah, and his mother still lived there. Often John would drive to Savannah on Friday evenings to spend the weekend with his mother, returning to Fernandina on Sunday evenings. On several occasions, he had car trouble and was forced to ride the bus, which would let him off at Yulee, Florida. I would drive the ten miles to Yulee to meet him and bring him back to Fernandina. Once, after I had met John at the bus stop and we were driving back on the dark, lonely road known as A1A, we noticed what appeared to be a single headlight coming up rapidly behind us. The light reflected in the rear view mirror and cast some light into the interior of the car. We decided that it was a motorcycle rider. John slowed down a little to allow the motorcycle rider to pass us, since the rider appeared to be in such a hurry. The light on the vehicle behind us slowed down as well. When John accelerated to normal driving speed once more, so did the following light. Suddenly the light vanished and we were alone on the road. Since there were no side roads along that stretch, we were mystified as to what had happened to the motorcycle. This same phenomenon occurred two other times on that same stretch of the A1A highway. We never mentioned it to anyone else for fear of ridicule, so there is no way of knowing if others had ever had the same experience.

It was while I was living in Fernandina that the second incident happened. John had gone to Pensacola for a job interview, and I was keeping his big standard poodle, Caesar. The apartment I rented was one of four in a building on the oceanfront. The apartment building, like so many others on the beach, was always rented in the summer, but after Labor Day stood empty, or at least nearly empty.

It was in October, and I was the only resident in the building. That evening after supper, I settled down with a book, intending to read until I got sleepy. Caesar was lying on the floor asleep near my feet. It was a quiet night, with a chill in the air. The sound of the breakers on the beach was soothing. The only other sounds were those of occasional cars driving down the street behind the building. Without warning, Caesar suddenly stood up, growling. I looked up from my book to see Caesar walking with stiffened gait across the room toward an inside corner of the apartment, still growling. I got up and walked over to him, placing my hand on his back. His entire body was rigid and stiff, and he was staring at the corner of the room, baring his teeth and growling. The whole atmosphere was eerie, and I felt the goose flesh rise on my arms. Caesar continued to hold this position for what seemed like hours, but in reality was probably only several minutes. Then he relaxed, and looked up at me. He walked back to the sofa, lay down, and went back to sleep, leaving me to wonder what he had seen.

Clearly something out of the ordinary had occurred. Caesar was not a nervous dog. His attitude toward his environment was what people today would describe as "laid-back." Nothing ever seemed to disturb his calm composure. This incident, therefore, was one that impressed itself on my consciousness. I knew that he had seen something, and whatever it was, it did not stay very long. It also never came back after that one incident.

Fernandina had its own share of unusual characters. The one I recall most vividly was a Negro man named Arthur. Arthur owned an ox and frequently drove his ox-cart on the quiet streets of the old fishing village. He scavenged food for his ox, and probably other things as well, from the dumpsters and trashcans. He was a familiar figure on the shady streets of the village, and quite a colorful individual.

Another interesting personality was Mrs. Stella Hutchins who owned the Seaside Hotel, a family-owned hotel right on the oceanfront. Although she appeared to be quite elderly at the time, she was probably only in her mid-sixties when I knew her. Mrs. Hutchins was an outspoken woman and highly opinionated. One of her sons operated a restaurant inside the hotel, while another son had a motel by the same name across the street. In addition to the usual summer tourists, she also rented a few rooms in the hotel to a handful of permanent residents, including John and a Florida Highway Patrolman named Sam Turnbull.

Most definitely a woman of strong convictions and a knack for making money, at one time Mrs. Hutchins and her husband, long deceased, had operated a casino in Fernandina. Those days were long past, however, and the Seaside Hotel was both her source of income and her home as well. She had her own private apartment located off the lobby, and little activity in the hotel escaped her notice. She had become a mother figure to the small number of single men she rented rooms to on a permanent basis, and she never hesitated to dispense advice to her tenants when she felt the need arise.

And Then There was Dora

September 9, 1964, was an auspicious day in the history of Amelia Island. In Fernandina, the school buses made their usual runs and disgorged children at the various schools, just another ordinary school day for students and the teachers. Labor Day had come and gone, and it was business as usual. The humdrum routine changed drastically by midmorning however, when school officials announced over the loudspeakers that busses would be arriving shortly and were to take all students home. Churning out in the Atlantic Ocean, almost due East of Amelia Island, was Hurricane Dora, and she seemed determined to strike the northeast Florida coast.

By noon, all children had been sent home, and teachers were dismissed as well. I went back to my apartment which was on the beach and which faced the ocean. It was not long before a Nassau County deputy came cruising down the beach highway with a loudspeaker telling residents that they needed to evacuate the island.

I packed most of my belongings into my car, and drove south to the Seaside Hotel to join John, who was also packing his things. When I went to the door, I met Mrs. Hutchins who informed me that she had no intention of evacuating. She had ridden out many storms in her two-story, red brick hotel, and Hurricane Dora was not going to alter her plans. John and I both, after unsuccessfully trying to persuade her to leave with us, decided that we could not drive off and leave her.

Mrs. Hutchins settled me in a room on the second floor, which had a lovely view of the ocean. Unfortunately, the ocean was not looking particularly lovely that day. With the business of a room out of the way, John and I began helping Mrs. Hutchins tape windows and move chairs from the front patio. As the afternoon wore on, a car arrived in the parking lot of the hotel, bearing two young college students who wanted a room. One of them was majoring in meteorology, while the other, Stu Sirroco, was studying journalism. Both had traveled to Miami, and had been following the storm up the Florida coast. As they traveled, one had been taking notes of a meteorological nature, while Stu was jotting down his impressions of the storm with the intention of selling his reports to various radio stations, by calling them in and reporting live. He then monitored the stations to see if they used his report. It was in this manner that he would be paid by the station.

The two young men joined us in helping to tape windows and doors against the coming storm. Two construction workers also showed up and lent a hand at securing the hotel as well. So there we were, seven very foolish individuals defying Hurricane Dora as the wind picked up considerably, and occasional gusts of rain hit the windows. The power failed in the afternoon, and Mrs. Hutchins pulled out some candles. A report from Stu's shortwave radio announced that Amelia Island had been completely evacuated. We laughed, knowing this was greatly exaggerated.

Our laughter faded however, when we heard a large vehicle pull up to the door of the hotel. Going to the door, we discovered a moving van had backed up to the door, and two men were getting out of the cab. Mrs. Hutchins stepped out and asked what they wanted. Neither man spoke, but jumped back into the van and drove away rapidly. They had also heard that the island had been evacuated, and they had decided that a little foray into the looting business was in order. They did not dream that an old lady and her entourage of six amateurs would thwart the looters' obvious intentions. The phone lines were down by now, and there was no way or reporting the looters.

Later, long after the hurricane had passed, we learned that some looters had been apprehended with quite a haul obtained from vacant homes on the island and along the coast.

As the wind began to blow in earnest, we were kept busy wiping up water that seeped through the windowpanes and around the edges of the doors. The roar of the surf and the howling wind lent a surrealistic air to the old hotel, which creaked and groaned with each fresh assault of nature. It would have been the perfect setting for a murder mystery. Stu Sirocco had similar thoughts as he composed a report and then used his short wave radio to contact a station. When he made a connection with a radio station, which agreed to use his story and pay him for it, he began reading his written account of the storm.

The eerie shadows cast by the candlelight was a fitting backdrop, with the appropriate sound effects of the raging storm in the background, as he began the broadcast with these words, "My name is Stu Sirocco and I am reporting live from the Seaside Hotel in Fernandina Beach. Writing this report by candlelight makes me feel like Mark Twain. As I speak, Hurricane Dora is wreaking havoc here. The water has reached the front doors, and we may be forced to move up to the second floor."

One of the construction workers, who were listening to the report with interest, looked up when he heard the words, "wreaking havoc." In a hushed and slightly awed voice he remarked, "If my daddy ever heard me use big words like that, he'd beat me over the head with a broomstick!"

Perhaps it is wise to comment here on Stu's observation that the water was reaching the front doors. Beside the Seaside was a ramp where cars could drive down onto the beach itself. During spring tides, the ocean would normally creep up the ramp to some extent. The night in question was nearly approaching the time for a spring tide. With the added effects of Dora, which pushed more water toward shore, the effect of the tide was amplified. Therefore, while his assessment of the water reaching the doors was essentially correct, the water did not actually threaten to come through the doors. We were spared this by several feet of sand and dune in front of the patio. The water flooding the ramp was never a threat to the building.

Hurricane Dora made landfall in the early hours of the morning, a direct hit on St. Augustine. Because we had pooled all of our provisions, we did not want for edibles. Mrs. Hutchins had built a small fire in the fireplace in the hotel lobby to ward off the dampness and chill. We all continue to mop up water from the driving rain that managed to seep in. Through it all, the wind blew unmercifully, and we watched a traffic light at the intersection beside the hotel spin around on its wire several times before it was blown down the street. We watched in awe as the wind carried a portion of the roof of the motel across the street and deposited it in the motel's swimming pool. The power of the wind had us in its spell, and the rain lashed the windows furiously.

By the following day, Dora, the only hurricane since the 1870s to make a direct hit on Florida's northeastern coast, had moved on. Although the wind was still blowing strongly, the sun was shining, and the devastation to the beach was plainly visible.

As we walked on the beach, we noticed that those houses built in more recent times had fared badly while the old beach shacks and cottages from the 30s and 40s made it through the storm none the worse for the wear. As we walked along, we heard the roar of a very low-flying plane, and looked up to see Air Force One with President Lyndon B. Johnson plainly visible, peering from the window of the plane at the storm damage. Storm related damage to Florida's east coast was estimated by some at $300 million dollars. Dora's name joined the ranks with Hurricane Hazel, and was forever retired from the official list of names for hurricanes by the U.S.

Meteorological Service

Mrs. Hutchins has passed on to her reward, as have her sons and daughter. The old Seaside Hotel still stands, a staunch sentinel at the intersection of South Fletcher Avenue and Sadler Road. Although it has changed little on the outside, the interior has been renovated in keeping with modern desires. Everything changes, and yet nothing really changes at all.

The Long Road Home

The story of Lieutenant Edward John Kent Johnston is a poignant one that serves to underscore the deep feelings that Southerners have for their land, and the conflict that that tore this nation apart in the years between 1861 and 1865. Perhaps this love is intensified because Lt. Johnston was gone from his beloved Southland for 139 years before he finally returned home.

Edward J. K. Johnston was born, of Scottish descent, in Dublin, Ireland, in 1827. In 1830, when he was only three years old, Johnston's family immigrated to America.

As a young man, Johnston traveled to Florida, and there in St. Augustine in 1852, he married Virginia Papy. The Johnstons eventually had four children, but when the War Between the States broke out, Edward Johnston went to Columbus, Georgia, where he enlisted in the Confederate Navy in 1861. After initially serving on the CSS *Baltic*, he attained the rank of Lieutenant and was reassigned in 1863 to the CSS *Atlanta* as Assistant Engineer.

On the 17th June of 1863, the CSS *Atlanta*, a Confederate ironclad, sailed from its mooring out into Wassaw Sound in Georgia with the intent of attacking the Federal ship USS *Weehawken* which was blockading the sound. During the ensuing battle between the two vessels, the *Atlanta* was run aground and captured by the *Weehawken*. The crew of the *Atlanta* was taken captive, and the CSS *Atlanta* was taken into the Union navy as the USS *Atlanta*.

Although the enlisted Confederate sailors were taken

prisoner, they were paroled a few weeks later and sent back to the South. Such was not the fate of the CSS *Atlanta*'s officers, including Lt. Johnston, who were taken to Ft. Lafayette in New York Harbor. They were later moved to Ft. Warren on Georges Island in Boston Harbor. There the men suffered from exposure, dysentery, poor clothing, and other problems faced by prisoners of war on both sides. Lt. Johnston contracted pneumonia and died at Ft. Warren on October 13, 1863. Johnston's fellow officers purchased a granite marker for $75.00 and saw to a proper burial for their comrade. According to Johnston's last wishes, he requested that he be buried with his face toward the South, and this wish was carried out. Mrs. Johnston and her children in Florida were never informed of his death. And so the years passed, with the grieving wife waiting for her husband to return, unaware that he was resting in a grave in Massachusetts.

Over time, a number of events disrupted the sleep of Lt. Johnston. Base closings, and shifts in military procedure, caused the United States government to move the remains of Lt. Johnston from Ft. Warren to Deer Island to Governor's Island and finally to Ft. Devens, Massachusetts.

In the meantime, one of Johnston's daughters had been researching federal records, looking for some mention of her father. She discovered that he had died in prison in Massachusetts, and had been buried there. In 1937, a granddaughter discovered that Mrs. Roscoe H. Chesley, who had founded a Chapter of the United Daughters of the Confederacy in Boston, had been placing flowers on Lt. Johnston's grave on every Memorial Day for the past seventeen years. There were no funds to bring Johnston's remains home to the South he loved and served so well.

The movement to take Lt. Johnston home was the brainchild of Mrs. Debbie Mattee, a native of Massachusetts who was involved with a living history event at Ft. Warren, and Mrs. Dana Chapman, a member of the Georgia Civil War

91

Commission. Their initial attempt ended before it even started when the two ladies learned from the Commander at Fort Devens that the remains could only be released to a family member. Consequently, a search was begun to locate an6y direct descendant of Johnston. After what seemed an interminable length of time, a great- great- grandson was located.

Assistance came from many different quarters as the efforts to bring home a Confederate soldier captured the imagination of a good portion of the nation. Mr. George Hagan, Jr., a Confederate naval re-enactor in Albany, Georgia, donated his time and money to cover all the costs, and along with members of various Sons of Confederate Veterans camps and the Florida Division of the United Daughters of the Confederacy, the project, begun in 1992, became a reality. Lt. Johnston was going home at last!

Massachusetts's officials, including the Governor of the state and the Massachusetts Highway Patrol, were on hand to view the solemn cortege as it left Ft. Devens. The State Police escorted the remains to the New York state line where New York Police took up the duty. Thus, slowly the remains traveled south, always under guard and escort, stopping only for the honor guard to sleep and eat, and even then a guard remained with the van. At each state line, an official escort, usually the State Police took up the task of escorting the remains to the next state.

On October 14, 2002, the procession passed through Savannah and made a brief stop at Old Fort Jackson where representatives of Savannah Chapter 2, UDC, and personnel at the fort met it. The re-enactors at Old Fort Jackson fired the cannon out across the Savannah River as a salute to Lt. Johnston. Within an hour or so, the procession had continued its journey south to Fernandina Beach, Florida.

On October 26, 2002, Lt. Edward J.K. Johnston was laid to rest in his family's plot in the old Bosque Bello Cemetery in

Fernandina. Thousands attended this last farewell, including SCV camps, UDC chapters, numerous dignitaries, and most touching of all, Johnston's great-great-grandson.

Lt. Edward John Kent Johnston now sleeps peacefully beneath an ancient live oak beside members of his family, his long journey home a reality at last.

The State of Chatham

Chatham County, Georgia, has always been an entity unto itself. Many states have counties that tend to be different to the extent of seeming apart from that state, and several of them refer to themselves as states. It takes a certain independence to act differently regardless of how the rest of the state functions. Many ways of accomplishing a set of goals are not always in line with dictates from Atlanta.

The State of Chatham, as Savannah is euphemistically referred to by people who find the ways and means of Savannahians incomprehensible at times, is a unique entity that often confuses newcomers to the point of befuddlement. Things are done a little differently in Savannah. Even the most dignified will listen sympathetically when newcomers vent their feelings about what is wrong with Savannah, and by association, the South as well. The nodding heads, the tsk-tsk-tsking, and the intense attention bestowed upon the unwary and the uninformed has the softening effect of assuring the complainer that one is well aware of such discrepancies, and it is really sad that newcomers have to cope with such inconsistencies and oddities.

For instance, Savannah is the only city where the train once backed into town. Few Savannahians, outside of those who are involved in some way with the railroads, really grasps *why* the train backed into town. It just did in Savannah, and therefore no further explanation is really necessary. That fact does not alter daily life in the least.

Savannah claims to be the home of an odd game called

"half rubber." Charleston disputes this claim, but then the two cities have enjoyed friendly rivalry since 1733. The game in question required three players, a rubber ball that had been cut in half, and a broomstick. It was played in the streets and lanes in the 1930s and 40s, and the rules varied from one game to the next. There was a pitcher, a catcher, and the batter. The ball was pitched and if the batter hit the ball, he remained up at bat until he missed. Three hits constituted a run, but no running actually occurred. When the batter missed hitting the ball, he was out, and the three players switched positions. Rules changed from game to game.

Another quirk has to do with some of the squares and the monuments in them. General Oglethorpe's statue is not in Oglethorpe Square, but instead stands proudly in Chippewa Square. Johnson Square is home to the Nathanael Greene monument, while Greene Square has no monument whatever. Monterey Square hosts Count Pulaski, while Pulaski Square has no statue. Now Savannahians do not concern themselves with these contradictions. That's the way it is, and that is the way it has always been. What is the problem with that? And, by the way, Lincoln Street was *not* named for Abraham Lincoln, either. It gets its name from Benjamin Lincoln, a Revolutionary hero.

Yes, we do have winos, vagrants, and their ilk warming the benches in some of our squares, and yes, there are laws against vagrancy, but we know some of them by name, and their eccentric behavior often earns them a permanent bench free of harassment by the police. For example, the black gentleman who weaves Confederate roses from palmetto fronds and sells them to tourists who frequently buy them out of some misguided notion that they are contributing to a cottage industry and at the same time are acquiring a bit of Southern history. In reality, these "roses," which received their name because young ladies made them and presented them to the young Confederates going off to war, often come undone and fall apart within a very short time. But, hey! It is an earnest attempt to pick up a little cash. *Caveat emptor*, y'all.

Don't look for Tara here either. There were never plantation homes in Savannah, because it was a city. Plantations were large farms, and of necessity were outside the city limits. While never that great in number, most of the old plantation homes caught the eye of the Yankee arsonist when he passed this way, and they are truly gone with the wind. Many of the old houses bore little resemblance to Tara, being large working farmhouses. There were a few exceptions, such as the pre-Revolution Mulberry Grove Plantation five miles upriver, but it was also burned. It was once the home of Revolutionary war hero, General Nathanael Greene, and it was there that Eli Whitney invented the cotton gin and revolutionized Southern economy. The only surviving plantation in the county is Wormsloe, but the original tabby house is long gone, the ruins of which are now part of the state park. The house that is there is privately owned and occupied by descendants of the original owner and is not open to tourists. In fact, you can only get a glimpse of it as you drive down the long avenue of stately old live oaks that line the entrance on your way to the state park property there.

The astute saxophone or guitar player who performs in various squares, depending on the time of day and the number of tourists, has an acute awareness of what tourists want to hear, and thus his repertoire consists of "Dixie," "When the Saints Go Marching In," and "Moon River." Monetary gifts of appreciation may be dropped in the hat or the guitar case, and earn the tourist a polite "Thank you, Suh," as the musician continues his impromptu concert.

The pigeon man who poses for photographs with dozens of pigeons adorning his arms and head offers another Kodak moment for tourists, who then seem nonplused when it is suggested that they contribute to the cause. Do they honestly believe that a man publicly entices pigeons to roost on him for the fun of it? And, by the way, we love our old cobblestone ramps that lead to the river. Those old ballast stones been around a lot longer than tourists. Yes, they make for a rather bumpy ride in a car, and they are very treacherous when wet. There are no plans to replace or pave over them, so if you are one of the fretful it is best to seek out alternate routes to the river.

Get real, people! Forrest Gump sat on so many benches in Chippewa Square that one can take his pick of whichever one has the background scenery that appeals to him. and, by the way, how many other places can boast of having an atomic bomb in Wassaw Sound, adjoining Tybee Island? We also occasionally have hurricanes that visit. We live dangerously here. Those who complain too loud and long about such things as cobblestones and narrow streets, and lack of public toilet facilities in the historic residential areas are reminded that I-95 still runs north, and access to it is relatively easy. Some Savannahians tend to take matters into their own hands and chart a course that, while adventuresome and dramatic, is doomed to ultimate failure. A case in point is Reds Helmey who hijacked a plane in January of 1969 and flew it to Cuba with the express purpose of assassinating Fidel Castro. This jaunt supposedly had the blessings of the CIA, but Helmey's imprisonment in Cuba, his return to Savannah, and a subsequent trial resulted in his acquittal on the grounds of temporary insanity.

Lest the reader gets an idea that we don't like tourists or Yankees, let me clarify our position. We love having tourists who come to view our elegant and unique city. They are our second largest industry. Only shipping outstrips them economically. As an addendum to the feelings toward Yankees, it is only those stereotypes who sometimes come to visit, and in loud, raucous tones, criticize our city that we dislike. If one takes the time to delve into genealogy, he would discover that many of Savannah's prominent families today have New

England roots. Savannah, being a seaport, invited all sorts of emigrants to settle here, the main drawing card being economic opportunity.

Savannah has been home to a substantial Jewish population since 1734. Mickve Israel Temple on Monterey Square has the distinction of being the only Jewish synagogue built in Gothic style architecture. I have been led to understand that some Northern folk dispute this claim, however, but then again, many New York Jews are of the opinion that Savannah Jews are not really Jewish. I wonder if this has anything to do with the Jewish food festival here in October. Their signature slogan is "Shalom, Y'all." Some of them also put up Christmas decorations, and at least one had membership not only at Temple Mickve Israel, but also in the Episcopal Church.

Earlier generations of Savannahians developed their own vocabulary. One still hears remnants of these colorful expressions, and they are frequently an endless source of amusement to outsiders. The one most often heard is used to establish veracity in someone telling a story. It is usually used in conjunction with the comment, "If you don't believe me," the remainder of the phrase being ..." I'll kiss your ass on Bull and Broughton." Now that is about as public as one can get, since the intersection of Bull and Broughton streets clearly delineates the center of town. Another expression, that to the best of my knowledge, is one that may have had its origins on the streets of Savannah, or it may be from my husband's rich store of quirky sayings. This saying, "Shit or go blind" may be akin to "Fish or cut bait." It is used when someone is caught in a state of intense indecision, and folks nearby get impatient with the soul searching of one who cannot make up his mind about something. I did see this particularly colorful bit of the Queen's English in print once. I believe it was in one of the "Prey" novels of John Sandford. I don't know if Sandford ever came to Savannah to pick up that naughty saying, or if he gleaned it from some other source. I believe that he did work

98

for a newspaper in Miami at some point in his highly successful career. Southerners don't mind borrowing phrases if it fits the need.

Still another memorable expression, seldom heard today, but one that was the favorite of a generation of young boys in the 1940s, few of whom had watches, was used when one of them was asked the time. The stock answer was, "Half past the cat's ass, quarter to his nuts." Now that is originality at its finest to be sure! A less innovative response was "Fifteen past the freckle."

In short, Savannah is Savannah in the State of Chatham, located in the northeast corner of Georgia. Who cares what the rest of the state, or world for that matter, thinks? This is Savannah, y'all, not Atlanta, or New York, or Chicago, or Los Angeles.

"Cap'n Sam"

Southerners love their local characters, and are not shy about speaking out about them in affectionate terms. Savannah is no exception, and sometimes seems to exert much time and energy to promoting them. One who exemplified outsiders' Hollywood concepts of the Old South was the indomitable Cap'n Sam, a colorful fixture on River Street who operated riverboat tours up and down the Savannah River for a number of years.

Born in Darien, Georgia, in 1912, Samuel L. Stevens was the son of a ship's carpenter. The Stevens family moved to Savannah about 1916, and young Sam grew up on the waterways that make up much of Chatham County. He completed his high school education, excelling in arithmetic and geography, and it seemed only natural that he would seek a career on the water. An older brother had obtained a position as steward on a passenger ship that traveled between Savannah and Baltimore in the 1920s. As a young teenager just out of high school, Samuel went to work for the U. S. Corps of Engineers and joined a crew of marine surveyors who were engaged in mapping and measuring the maze of mountain streams in North Carolina that meandered throughout the highlands and eventually merged to form the Savannah River. His job had the designation of Surveyor Assistant.

When the United States entered World War II, Samuel joined the United States Coast Guard in 1942 as Fireman First Class. His stint in the Coast Guard lasted nine years, most of which was spent in local waters. By the time he finally left the service in the Coast Guard, he had obtained the rank of Master Machinist First Class.

After leaving the Coast Guard, Stevens was not inclined to go back to work with the Corps. Instead, he chose to go into business for himself. His choice was the fuel oil business, but the pull of Savannah's waterways was strong, and Stevens' lifelong dream was to have a vessel of his own.

The opportunity to realize this dream came in March of 1952 when an excursion steamer, *The Visitor*, owned by the Circle Line of New York was retired from active commercial transport and passenger service and was put up for sale. Forming a partnership with two local doctors, Collier and McDew, Stevens named the enterprise the CMS Steamship Lines and purchased *The Visitor*, piloting it down the Atlantic coast to its new berth in Savannah.

The Visitor no sooner arrived in Savannah than it was put into almost immediate operation as a riverfront tour boat. Regular tours of Savannah's waterfront, and special charter trips to nearby locations such as Daufuskie Island made *The Visitor* popular not only with tourists, but with the local citizens as well. On a sadder note, there were many trips to Daufuskie made by black families who frequently chartered the boat either to attend family funerals or to carry a coffin to its final destination in one of the many family-owned burial plots on Daufuskie. Stevens also began regularly scheduled shopping shuttles between Daufuskie and Savannah for the islanders. Round trip fare was four dollars.

Cap'n Sam's entrepreneurial endeavor claimed national coverage as *Life* magazine and *Ebony* both devoted editorial and pictorial coverage to this new business. Although it took nearly twelve years for this enterprise to show a profit, Cap'n Sam very early bought out Dr. McDew's interest in the CMS Lines.

In 1972, the popularity of Steven's harbor tours had outgrown *The Visitor*. He began looking for another boat. He heard about a boat called the *Fair Maid* that suited his purposes. The *Fair Maid* was brought to Savannah and renamed *The Waving Girl*. This new craft was an instant success. By 1978, Stevens had acquired the *Harbor Queen, Harbor Queen II,* and the *Cap'n Sam.*

Sam was not only a riverboat captain, but a family man as well. He and his wife Leola had two daughters, Constance and Theresa, and a son, Robert Lee Stevens. He also served on the deacons' and trustees' boards of the First African Baptist Church in Savannah.

Nevertheless, all good things must come to an end. In the 1980s Stevens, faced Federal charges that he had defrauded the United States government of fuel oil through Stevens Oil Company. A federal jury convicted him of the charges in June of 1989, and Cap'n Sam was sentenced to federal prison. He was incarcerated in Fort Worth, Texas, at a federal prison-medical facility, suffering from several medical conditions. His cruise business and the oil business went bankrupt in 1990. It was while in prison that Stevens had two strokes. His Savannah attorneys petitioned the U. S. District Judge for the 80-year-old's early release due to deteriorating health problems, which included hypertension, heart failure, glaucoma, and prostate cancer, in addition to effects of the two strokes. Because of the esteem in which he was held in Savannah, the early release was affected and Cap'n Sam came home to Savannah in April of 1992.

Due to his failing health, brought on by the two strokes while he was incarcerated, Cap'n Sam was placed in a nursing home. He died at Candler General Hospital on July 29, 1992, at the age of 80. Thus, a chapter on one of Savannah's legendary personalities closed with little fanfare.

Indian Albert

I first heard of Indian Albert when I was interviewing Mr. Stephen Williams one afternoon at Massey School. I was helping to put together an exhibit that was to show two hundred years of education in Savannah, and I had come across an article in a recent issue of the newspaper, which mentioned Mr. Williams in connection with the Haven Home School, a private boarding school for blacks, which once stood on Montgomery Crossroads. Bartlett Middle School currently occupies the site of that early school. The site was also one that once had a very large Indian mound, shown on early maps as the "Indian King's Tomb."

Wylly Albert Reed Ann Belton" was born near Richmond, Virginia, about 1839. She claimed to be the daughter of an Indian mother, and by her own admission, she referred to herself as a mulatto, though she claimed Indian and Chinese as the principal strains of blood in her veins. As an infant, she and her mother were sold into slavery. When she was about 20 years old, she was freed. She made her way to Mississippi and lived near Meridian, Mississippi, until about 1915. At that time, she left Mississippi and wandered into Florida, going as far as Miami.

From Miami she made her way to Savannah and there she decided to stay. After living for a while in various parts of Chatham County, including Pooler and then later in Sandfly, she drifted on foot to Montgomery Crossroads. She supported herself by collecting old newspapers, rags, cans, and miscellaneous items to sell. Her other means of earning money

103

was her ability to stand on her head in return for donations of small change from the spectators.

Margaret Ryals Scott, who was born in the little town of Clyo, in Effingham County, Georgia, in 1916, says that she can remember coming with her aunts in a Model T Ford and riding down Bay Street. Near the intersection of Fair Street with Bay Street, where the health center is now there used to be small wooden huts built of the rough boards from the sawmill. There was a dirt road lined with large old oak trees that led down to the river. It was in this area that she remembers seeing Indian Albert. Mrs. Scott, who was six or seven years old at the time, tells how amazed she was to see this strange looking woman with a reddish complexion, standing on her head. To a young child this must have been an unforgettable experience.

This was Albert's chief claim to fame. From this dubious talent, and her scavenging enterprises, she managed to save enough money to buy two pieces of county property. One of these pieces of property was on White Bluff Road, near Montgomery Crossroads. The other was near Isle of Hope. She evidently reveled in her reputation for eccentricity. The only times she actually came into Savannah occurred once a year when she donned a burlap skirt over her pantaloons and came in to the courthouse where she paid her property taxes.

Albert, in her more youthful days, was a hard worker, and particularly enjoyed chopping down trees or laboring in the fields, those jobs most folks considered a man's work. One she attempted to lift the corner of a building, and in doing so, injured her back in such a way that thereafter she walked with a stooped gait. This injury, however, did not seem to affect her ability to stand on her head.

Sunday afternoons often found many local residents motoring out to her tiny hut to watch her perform. Albert had offered to stand on her head for an hour for the sum of $100, but there were no takers from the groups of people who gathered to watch the lady in pantaloons agilely flip her body up until she was standing on her head. She was known to the local population as "Indian Albert," or sometimes as "Mom Albert." This last sobriquet referred to her reputation for kindness. According to reports, she took food and clothing to the elderly and needy, and often spent some of the money she earned to help others. Her sole companion was a little white, shaggy-haired terrier that she called "Busy."

In August of 1933, Albert's tiny thatched-roof house near Montgomery Crossroads suddenly caved in from a collapsing roof. This destruction of her home was apparently due to the effects of recent heavy rains that soaked the old timbers thereby increasing their weight. Coupled with weakening foundations and underpinnings, the structure finally gave way and fell. At the time, Albert was away from home, on one of her scavenging expeditions. Returning home, she took the loss of her dwelling in stride and she began sifting through the rubble to salvage what she could of her possessions. She then moved her residence to her second home located near Isle of Hope.

On Friday, January 4, 1935, Albert failed to appear in her usual haunts. Concerned neighbors investigated and found Albert's lifeless body in her tiny hut. According to reports by the newspaper, she was discovered stretched out on a crude wooden pallet with her arm resting in a box of soda crackers. Initially, rumors spread that Albert was the victim of foul play, that she had been robbed and murdered, but after examination by the coroner, her death was attributed to Bright's disease. A local mortician, Monroe Undertaking Company, took her body away to prepare it for burial.

A sad note to the story concerns her little terrier, "Busy." Busy took up a position at the front door of the modest house. There the faithful little dog waited for his master, not knowing that Albert would never return. He snarled when people approached the house. The neighbors tried to feed the dog, but Busy refused food. No record seems to exist which indicates the fate of Busy. However, Indian Albert, in spite of her eccentric nature, was astute enough to leave a handwritten will. This was a crude, pencil-written document. It contained exactly thirteen words:

"Savannah, Ga., September 10, 1934, I Albert, will all I die possessed of to Melvin and Irene Slack."

It was signed: "Wylly A. R. A. Belton," and was properly witnessed by Mrs. D.O. Carter, Frank R. Ragsdale and Mrs. Frank R. Ragsdale.

This document was filed for probate in the Court of the Ordinary of Chatham County,

Georgia. Indian Albert's estate consisted of two pieces of real estate and a savings account in a local bank.

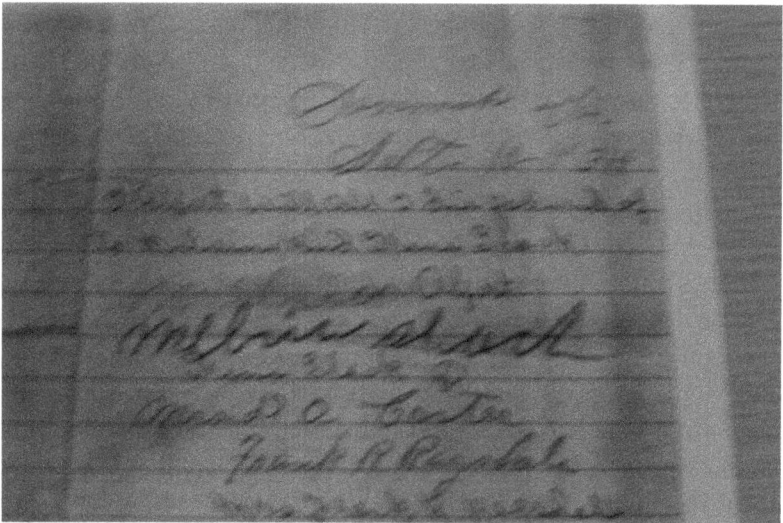

Indian Albert's Will

106

Witch Doctor or Healer?

Tales of root doctors, conjure women, and spells that cause an enemy to wither and die abound in the South. In truth, however, such practices are much less dramatic than implied by the stories. Voodoo, a religion brought by African slaves to the United States in the early 1800s, is the dominant religion of Haiti today, and is composed of African spirit worship and Catholicism. It is concerned with healing, foretelling the future, interpreting dreams, casting spells, and appeasing the spirits. Ceremonies are usually held outdoors and often include animal sacrifice. Most forms of voodoo are benign, but occasionally it may encompass what we often refer to as black magic.

In this country, little if any remnant of voodoo worship is prevalent today. It, along with so many customs and practices, appears to have faded away, leaving in its path vague recollections of another time and place. Shutters and doors of small cottages may still be painted "haint" blue, but the basic premise behind this practice has been lost or romanticized by homebuyers who continue the use of "haint" blue thinking they are reviving an old Southern custom. The actually practice of painting shutters this distinct color came from the old belief that malevolent spirits could not cross water, which is what "haint" blue represents. It therefore followed the belief that if you painted shutters and doors this color, then no malign spirits would be able to enter the dwelling. Today, it is merely a quaint decorative novelty.

On the other hand, the old root doctors in Savannah did hold a position of esteem within their immediate community.

Often lacking easy access to medical attention, many poorer citizens turned to those in their neighborhood who might be able to offer some sort of remedy for their medical needs. These root doctors were skilled in the use of herbs, spirit readings, and prayer to help many who turned to them. While the root doctors were revered, they were also often feared. Quite often, defying all odds, they were often successful in their efforts to heal. Savannah had its share of root doctors, but in some instances, they may have had their own dark secrets and were less than reputable.

A case in point is that of Lou Assan Orjuna, a 68 year-old black man who was living in Savannah in 1958.The story was reported in the *Savannah Morning News* August 8, 1958. Orjuna's life, according to him, was one of extraordinary contradictions. He was a native of Jamaica in the British West Indies, and claimed to be a practitioner of voodoo and in the use of native remedies for healing. He further claimed that he had studied biology at Oxford University in England from 1913 to 1916 where he had enrolled under the name Sam Jenkins. From 1940 until 1944, he claimed that he had been enrolled at College of Divine Metaphysics and Naturopathy in Indianapolis, Indiana.

Apparently, Orjuna traveled extensively, and he eventually found his way to Homestead, Florida. In 1950, Orjuna was alleged to have engaged in a physical confrontation with the Reverend Osmund J. McLeod, an Episcopal priest, near some railroad tracks. A fight ensued, and Orjuna, with the help of two others, dragged the Reverend McLeod's body onto the tracks where he was run over by a train. Orjuna was tried and convicted of murder in January 1953, and was given a life sentence at Raiford. He escaped in 1957, and came to Savannah. He found a place to live on West 41st Street and began practicing spiritual reading in and around Savannah. Orjuna had disguised himself by darkening his gray hair. This made him appear to be twenty years younger. He was described by various people as "a suave character of the con man variety." He used several aliases, but operated in Savannah under the name Reverend R. S. Ferguson. He described himself as a "witch doctor" and a voodoo specialist. He considered himself a spiritual reader and a healer.

When the F.B.I. arrested Orjuna on a warrant charging him with unlawful flight to avoid confinement, he surrendered to police and the F.B.I. peacefully. He was returned to Florida to continue his sentence at Raiford State Prison.

Ties That Bind

When people from other places think about this fabled, mystical land that is located south of an equally mystical line known as the Mason-Dixon Line, at some point in their thought processes, the question of the enslavement of Africans arises. To many in northern climes, the South was a land of Taras, hoopskirts, mint juleps or bourbon and branch water, and people whose speech was liberally sprinkled with "y'alls." Smiling mammies tended their young white charges and took liberties with their white mistresses that frequently bordered on insolence.

The reality, most assuredly absent from this idyllic picture, is quite another story. Yes, there were slaves in the South, and some in the North as well. Some did live rather favored, languid lives, while others toiled long, hot hours on the land. Not all slaves, however, had white masters. A significant number of free black men and women owned slaves. Savannah had a relatively large free black population, and some of these were slave owners. In the aftermath of the war, they lost as much as their white counterparts, but their history has often been brushed aside. Few today, black or white, are even aware that black slave owners existed, or that they held a favored place in society.

When General Sherman, that red-headed arsonist, arrived in Savannah in December of 1864, one of his directives issued at the Second African Baptist Church on Greene Square made the spurious promise of "Forty acres and a mule" to each freed slave. This was a promise that he could not keep, nor did he

110

pay much attention to the aftermath of this Field Order. He had set his face on that hotbed of insurrection, the indomitable South Carolina, and Savannah was just a stopping off place to catch his breath after the long march from Atlanta to the sea. Presenting Savannah to President Lincoln as a Christmas present was a calculated media play. Sherman had his eyes on bringing South Carolina to her knees, and he did not waste much time with the plight of the freed slaves who followed his army.

In fact, though many former slaves were given a deed to acreage, it was not necessarily forty acres, nor was it often prime land. There were stipulations attached which stated that the acreage must be put into cultivation. Many slaves who had worked the land for their masters were frequently not too thrilled to be offered land, which needed cultivating – they had had their share of farm labor. As a result, much of the offered acreage was not claimed. Industrious blacks who carved out a living for themselves, raising vegetables and some livestock, settled the properties that were officially granted to former slaves who were willing to work the land. Some of them established successful small farms, while others earned a living from the waters that abutted their properties, such as those at Pin Point, Isle of Hope, Montgomery, Sandfly, and other small river communities. Today, many of the descendants of these former slaves still live on land given to their ancestors. Most of these, however, are part of an aging population, the younger generations having long moved out and on to other places and careers.

Regrettably, much of this land today is prime real estate. Some of it is waterfront property. County taxes continue to rise and it becomes harder to hold onto the land. Some are being forced to sell their heritage due to the voracious appetites of investors who want to develop these properties for wealthy buyers. Once again, the old families are being uprooted so that newcomers can have a luxurious home with a view.

A case in point is that of John R."Jack" Stiles, Jr. of Sandfly, Georgia. Born January 14, 1914, the son of John R. and Lucille Stiles, Jack Stiles was 87 years old when a friend, Allison Thurlow, and I interviewed him in August of 2001. He is a retired electrical contractor. Confined to wheelchair for the past 51 years, he was nevertheless a pleasant, well-read gentleman, who had received an education at Hampton Institute in Hampton, Virginia. His well kept home was full of books arranged neatly on built-in shelves, and also stacked on tables within easy reach of his wheelchair.

John R."Jack" Stiles, Jr.

Mr. Stiles had no compunction about talking about his ancestors. Obviously, he was well-informed about his family history, and not averse to discussing it dispassionately with two white women who had come to his home hoping to gain some insight into the psyche of a man who could recite his family background without feeling defensive or threatened. His factual account is quoted directly from that interview:

My name is John R. Stiles, Jr. I was born 87 years ago. I have been in this wheelchair for 51 years. My parents were Savannahians.

My mother's people came from Durham, North Carolina, but I don't know much about them. My family, the Stiles family, came to Savannah in 1769 from Bermuda. Their plantation was on the Ogeechee River.

All of my grandfolks were enslaved and I do not know much about them because my family didn't talk much about them.

My great grandfather was Benjamin Stiles, a white British man who was from Bermuda where he had a mulatto breeding farm. It was said that he had 26 children by two slave sisters. There was nothing unusual about that. It was a common practice. I don't know if he claimed those children as his own, but he did look after them.

Slavery was not legalized until 1750. There was not supposed to be slavery in Georgia, but South Carolina did permit slaves. George Whitfield brought his slaves over the river and carried them back every night. Sir Wimberly Jones had the first legalized slaves in Savannah, in Chatham County. After the War, they had some land on Skidaway Island, but it went back to the old owners and most of the people were run off the island – Skidaway Island, Pin Point, Sandfly people, I mean.

Most of them came to Sandfly, a settlement that dates back to 1740 when Bethesda was started. They either worked for Wimberly Jones at Wormsloe, later owned by DeRenne and then Barrow. All of these were originally the Jones family.

Sandfly, as a community, did not really get started until after 1865.

People say they did have slaves here, but there is no record of that. They probably did have – everybody had slaves – well, not everybody, because some people couldn't afford not even one slave. Slaves were very expensive. There are more blacks in Pin Point than they have in Sandfly.

These people out here were very superstitious. They believed in roots, conjure. There are still some folks that believe in it. They believe in spirits – that type of thing. Conjure. You go over and get some cemetery dirt, mix with some hair, meal, and put it is a little bag and bury it in your yard. They still believe that. That's some of their culture they brought from Africa.

They believe in drums, and a lot of the plantations owners stopped them from using drums because they were able to communicate. Boom-boom-boom-boom. And they would talk.

I think some people still living on Sapelo Island know how to make the drums talk. You see the whites were afraid of the drums, because they were afraid there would be an uprising. That's the one thing they feared.

Even in their churches, when they allowed the blacks to preach to the blacks, a white man was there to make sure that they didn't say anything about freedom.

LaPageville out on Wheaton Street was where they found the cemetery and tried to preserve it. That's in the Fort. My mother was born in the Fort. There are only two places to be born in Savannah, the Fort and Yamacraw – Old Fort. I'm an electrical contractor, and I used to go through there and wire those shacks, those little two room shacks – Tin City – made out of tin – whatever they could scrape up.

The Irish lived in Old Fort, but they were restricted. They put them down there with the blacks, understand, but after dark they couldn't cross Habersham Street. I remember the Irish sweeping the side streets in Savannah with a push broom. Shanty Irish. They gave 'em a hard time. And that's how we got so mixed up. That's why they got all them light colored people. St. Matthew's Church was designed purposely.

I mean the first one, where all the white folks went, on Habersham Street. They were very upset when the bishop said they had to join the churches.

They had the black church on West Broad Street, Father Riley, an Episcopal church, but that church was created so that the mulattos, the light colored didn't have to go to church with the black folks. Being a mulatto was a definite advantage. I remember reading in the Savannah Evening Press want ads, 'Would like a maid, nice-looking, light-skinned, colored girl'. You understand.

Jack Stiles passed away on July 6, 2007 at Hospice of Savannah. In lieu of a funeral, his large family chose to celebrate his long life with a memorial service at the family home in Sandfly.

Savannah has long been noted for its ghost stories, a few of which lay claim to factual accounts, and others of extremely dubious origin. Many of these have been written about, and recounted and embellished regularly by tour guides escorting their clients throughout the historic district of the city. In fact, many of the ones heard by tourists today were made up on the spot, or at best are of recent manufacture. This can be explained by the fact that many of the ghost tour guides are not native Savannahians, and have little understanding of the events they love to relate. The best stories, however, are those which are not so publicized and which are generally only related from time to time with friends over dinner or a cocktail. Stories of this nature are certainly more credible, as the narrator has little to gain from the telling, other than a reputation for being a little "odd" by the unbelievers and the skeptics.

My husband John spent the early years of his life growing

115

up in a house on the corner of Jones and Lincoln Streets. This was a house built of Savannah gray brick, those lovely, locally made bricks of another era. The house was constructed in the two floors above an English basement manner. The kitchen was located in the basement and contained a fireplace from earlier days. The house itself was used as a movie set during the filming of "Something To Talk About."

John lived here with his mother, father, and other occasional family members, including his Aunt Julia. Aunt Julia's bedroom was on the second floor, which was actually the third floor above street level. Her room contained a fireplace that was connected to the one in the kitchen, two floors below. From the beginning, Julia's sleep was frequently disturbed by the appearance of a man wearing a suit who materialized rather regularly in the vicinity of the fireplace. At first, being a person with a no-nonsense attitude toward life in general, Julia attributed this vision to an annoying dream. She was well aware that what she was seeing was not a real person. Gradually however, she began to realize that she was not the only one to witness this apparition.

Annie, a Negro cook in the house, encountered the same figure stepping out in front of the kitchen fireplace. She too ignored it the first time, but subsequent appearances upset her to the point that she threatened to quit. It soon became obvious that something should be done, and soon.

Mr. and Mrs. Piechocinski, being parishioners of the Cathedral of St. John the Baptist, decided that a priest should intervene in the matter. Accordingly, a priest of the church came to their house and went from room to room, conducting a blessing ceremony in each room of the house, from basement to attic. The strange appearances ceased, and the man in the suit apparently moved on to other pastures.

Similar ceremonies have taken place in other homes in Savannah, and indeed, elsewhere. They are seldom publicized, as many people still believe that it is not necessary to open locked closets for the general public's consumption. Their stories are all the more credible by an innate desire to keep the story in the family, or at least among friends. They do not wish to invite hordes of curiosity seekers into their homes, and thus the events become part of that family's history and lore. Old Southern families, in general, do not believe that their family's private matters need to be publicized and exploited by local entrepreneurs seeking a quick buck. For this reason, many of the best stories have not been told.

While I was researching a previous book, a local businessman who owned a blueprint company told me of a strange recurring phenomenon at his office. The main floor of his business was where supplies were kept and sold, and where blueprints and related documents were prepared. There was a small second floor room used to store various materials. He had a client who was anxious to get some documents that were being prepared for him, and so he informed that client that if he came to the office on Sunday afternoon the documents would be ready. When the client arrived, George went to the back of the building to get the documents and papers for his client. Soon George heard the client calling to him, "Hey, George, your little girl wants you." This was puzzling, because George did not have a little girl, or any children for that matter. Coming from the back of the building, George questioned the client and learned that a little girl with curly hair appeared on the narrow stairs, calling, "Daddy, Daddy?"

This occurred on several different occasions, but no explanation seemed adequate. It was later, in the course of my research that I came across an item in an early Savannah newspaper about a doctor whose wife had died of fever, leaving him with several small children, including a little girl. The little girl became ill and died. The doctor's office was located on the site where George's modern building stands today.

There was also another doctor whose office was the near

this site. Dr. Mary Lavinder, an early woman doctor who treated primarily women and children, had her office on York Street. She treated many yellow fever victims there at her office, and it was here that she died in 1845. No record of where she is buried exists, but a tribute to her appeared in an early newspaper. While the place and date of her death suggest a burial in Colonial Cemetery, there are other possible locations, one of which is no longer in existence. This site is the old Lavinder Cemetery, also known as 76 Cemetery, that was once located on the site of the athletic field at Herschel V. Jenkins High School. There were upwards of sixty gravesites there, and according to legal documents, the graveyard was to be excluded from the sale of the property in the 1950s. This exclusion was blatantly and illegally ignored by Board of Education at that time, the stones were discarded, and the old cemetery leveled and partially paved.

Descendants of those buried in the old Lavinder cemetery are currently trying to recover the tombstones, and have contemplated erecting a tablet acknowledging the cemetery's existence. Whatever measures may eventually be taken will no doubt stir up old scandals and old grudges. An examination of the rather thick file, which contains a number of legal documents and letters from one attorney to another places the Board of Education in a distinctly unflattering light.

Presently, there is an attempt to encourage the Board of Education to recognize the Lavinder Cemetery. There is talk of possibly erecting a monument with the names of those buried there whose graves were bulldozed and markers removed with little thought or respect for an old burial ground. In fact, I was recently told that a monument has been erected on the site, and that it lists the names of the known burials on that property. At least there is some closure to this controversial topic.

That Other House on St. Julian Street

Claims that Savannah is possibly the most haunted city in America may be pure tourist hype, but that is not to say that strange things don't happen in this old colonial capital of Georgia. St. Julian Street is the location of the old Hampton-Lillibridge house, reputed to be the most haunted house in the city. However, that is not the only house on St. Julian Street that has seen its share of mysterious, perhaps ghostly, activity.

Several years ago, I was asked to create an exhibit covering 200 years of education in Savannah for the Massie Heritage Center. In the course of researching materials for use in the exhibit, I decided that I needed to include information on Jane Deveaux, a black woman who educated black children when such action was illegal, according to Georgia law forbidding the education of slaves.

Jane Deveaux's history is a fascinating one. The daughter of a pastor of the Second African Baptist Church on Greene Square, she had been sent up North for an education. She returned to Savannah in 1847, and moved into a small house on Price Street owned by Henry Willink where she began holding clandestine classes, teaching black children, both free and slave, in her home. When civil patrols raided places where it was believed that slaves were learning to read, Jane would send the children up into the loft of her little cottage, warn them to be very quiet and still, and close the trap door. When the patrols entered her house, they would find Miss Deveaux busy at some household task. She was never caught, and there are many who believe that sympathetic local citizens were aware of her illegal school and that they often sent her advance notice when the patrols were checking the area for such illegal activities. Her secret school lasted until 1865.

The little cottage, built for Henry F. Willink in 1845 as income property, was originally located on Price Street south of Oglethorpe Avenue in what is today the Beech Institute neighborhood. The little cottage was moved sometime in the 1960s to the northwest corner of St. Julian Street and Price Street. There is no legal record or document that states that Henry F. Willink ever lived in this house. Indeed, early city directories indicate that Henry Willink lived on the northwest corner of Oglethorpe Avenue and Habersham Street.

The Other House of Julian Street

Today, this neat little house, surrounded by a white picket fence, is home to Mrs. D., a retired principal of a private school in Savannah. She purchased the house in 1976. Prior to that time, it had belonged to the Lanes who used it as a guesthouse, and then later as an office. Recently, I spoke with Mrs. D. on the phone and asked her about the stories she had told me on that earlier visit. She was quite willing for me to use the stories, but did ask that I not use her real name. When I had the opportunity to go into the house and to talk with her, I was treated to four interesting stories of incidents that occurred in the house since the owner has lived there.

On that visit to Mrs. D's. house, she led me up the narrow staircase to the door that opens into a spacious loft, which is now her bedroom and bath. One of the windows faces the rear of the house and because it is part of a deep gable has a very deep sill. Sitting on the windowsill was a very large potted plant in a very heavy clay urn. Mrs. D. pointed out the large plant and told me that her first indication that things were not quite as they seemed came when her maid called her at school one day and insisted that she come home immediately. The maid had been in the bedroom cleaning when the plant, pot and all, rose up in the air and then plunked down. This happened several times, with no visible cause in sight. Terrified, the maid made a hasty retreat downstairs to call her employer. Although, no explanation for the strange occurrence could be found, Mrs. D. attributed the odd event to heavy traffic outside, or perhaps even a slight earth tremor. However, she was startled the next day to find that her plant, which she had carefully nurtured for several years, had died overnight.

A second incident took place one evening. Mrs. D. had retired for the night and was in her bed watching television, her small dog at her feet. Suddenly, her dog perked up its ears, jumped off the bed, and ran to the closed door to the steps and growled. Footsteps sounded on the stairs, as the dog continued to growl. Mrs. D. was startled, but then she came to the realization that she was helpless to defend herself against the unknown intruder. She listened as the footsteps reached her bedroom door, as her dog continued to growl. Then came a dead silence. After several seconds, Mrs. D. got out of bed, and walked to the door. Taking a deep breath, she cautiously opened the door, and peered out down the stairs. There was nothing there! Gathering up her courage, she bravely descended the stairs. Nothing was amiss below. All of the doors were locked, and none of the windows were open, nor had any been disturbed. Despite, the earlier frightening experience, Mrs. D. returned to her bedroom, where she slept undisturbed the rest of the night.

The third incident was a relatively insignificant thing at first. Mrs. D. had placed a wooden bowl of nuts on a table near the fireplace in her living room. One day she noticed that the nuts had been removed from the bowl and were on the floor in a pattern forming a perfect circle. Another time she found the nuts scattered on the floor, and yet another time they were arranged in a different pattern. There seemed to be no logical explanation to this.

The fourth incident Mrs. D. related to me concerned a time when she and her daughter who was visiting her had gone grocery shopping. Returning home, she pulled her car into the small parking area behind the house. Her daughter got out of the car and filled her arms with bags of groceries. As her daughter approached the back door, it suddenly opened for her, although the door had been locked when she left, and she had not had time to fumble for the key because her hands were full. Mrs. D.'s daughter walked into the tiny kitchen, automatically saying, "Thank you," as she entered the house. Both women assumed that the unknown presence was just being mannerly.

While popular ghost story writers have suggested that Capt. Henry Willink, whose wife supposedly drowned while helping him on a ship he was building, leaves the house and walks down to the wharf at night, there is a serious problem with Willink being the restless spirit in Mrs. D.'s house. As was stated earlier, the fact is that while Willink had the house built in 1845, there is no indication that he ever lived in the house. It is extremely tiny for a man and his wife, and perhaps children as well. It appears to have been specifically designed for single occupancy. It is also not located on its original site.

Mrs. D. told me that she had developed a very real antipathy toward tourists who have knocked on her door and wanted to come in and look at a "real' haunted house. There are others who have wanted to know if "real people" live in the haunted houses in Savannah. Evidently, for many such visitors, Savannah has become a movie set to entertain the masses. At any rate, Mrs. D., who is 87 years old, has little patience with such requests and questions that reflect tales told by unscrupulous ghost tour companies. A mild-mannered Southern lady, she values her quiet life, and does not take kindly to insensitive visitors who feel her house should be open to the public.

Their questions are abhorrent to her, as they seem to indicate a lack of good breeding and manners. Her house is a private residence, and private property is still respected in the South, although there are always those individuals who believe that they have the right to trespass on such property if they so desire.

The Battle of the Bathtubs

Savannah is known for its oddities and quirks, but the battle of the bathtubs surely deserves a place in the history of this illustrious old city. The stories surrounding this particularly noteworthy event were found in the pages of the *Savannah Morning News* for June 19, 19–. The setting for this "story" begins at 312 East Bryan Street, but soon is moved to the northeast corner of Broughton and Habersham streets.

The house that stood at 312 East Bryan Street was built about 1800. Over the ensuing years, it was occupied by a number of different owners. During the terrible yellow fever epidemic that swept the city, a physician by the name of John F. Posey had taken a prominent role in tending to the sick during that frightening and devastating epidemic that decimated a significant portion of the population. It was this man whose efforts to provide a comfortable home for his new wife unwittingly became the source for a later dispute.

Dr. Posey married Mary Haupt on October 13, 1838, and it was to the house at 312 East Bryan Street that he brought his bride. Shortly after the couple had settled in their new home, the Posey's had one of the new-fangled bathtubs installed in the house. Thus, the house at 312 East Bryan was given the distinction of having the first bathtub in the city of Savannah.

This innovation apparently caught the imagination and interest of the citizens of Savannah, particularly among the young boys who lived in the area. According to the story, young boys would stop at the house at all hours of the day, begging and pleading with Mrs. Posey to let them take a bath.

Today, this story about little boys begging to take a bath would be highly implausible to say the least. I rather imagine that perhaps these young boys discovered an innovative way to while away their days in a city that probably was lacking in activities to entertain the young.

In the meantime, another house in Savannah challenged the claim of being the first in the city to have a bathtub installed. William Gaston built the Col. Charles Lamar home on the northeast corner of Habersham and Broughton streets in the early 1800s. Col. Lamar gave the house to one of his daughters as a wedding present. The tub was installed about 1840. Numerous Lamar family members insisted that it was this house that had the first bathtub in Savannah.

The writer of the newspaper story interrupts his narrative to explain the degree of difference between a bath and a bathtub, as opposed to a shower. According to him, a "bath" would have been the proper term used to designate one made of marble. A 'bathtub" would have been one of the newfangled rare gadgets made of iron or tin. In later years, the metal tub would have been covered over with porcelain. According to him, "shower people" don't have much to do with "tub people."

Because some members of the Savannah Bar Association backed the claim by the Lamar family that their house had the first bathtub in Savannah, local tradition tended to give credit to the Col. Lamar house rather than Dr. Posy's house. Tongue in cheek, the writer of the story commented that the Savannah Bar no doubt had a long familiarity with such things as the history of bathtubs. As is often the case, as far as Savannah is concerned, if enough people say the same thing often enough, it eventually becomes touted as fact. This is not the first time that public opinion has replaced fact.

Regardless of which claim to fame is correct, this story merely points out the importance of being first in anything, no matter how trivial. It also underscores the fact that Savannah was a pioneer in household conveniences. Along with other firsts, Savannah also claims to have the first golf course in the United States. Charleston disputes this particular claim vigorously. The Savannah Bar has not handed down a ruling on this yet.

The Old Gray Mule

One of the most fascinating parts of researching material for the various books I have written is the unusual information I sometimes inadvertently uncover in the process.

Since I often go to old newspaper files and stories, I frequently am sidetracked as I peruse an interesting story that has no discernible connection with the topic I am researching. Newspapers of a bygone era tended to publish more interesting items that were written with skills utilized by good storytellers. Older newspapers included much detail and considered the sensational events that occurred in everyday life worth reporting. This style is seldom found in modern newspapers, which are more concise and much less picturesque in their versions of reportable facts. So much of our human-interest stories are devoid of any emotion on the part of the writer, tending to be a rendition of bare facts composed in a very dry and, all too often, inaccurate manner. Nothing is included to excite the imagination. This modern pattern or style of journalism was not always the norm however, as evidenced by the following account:

The evening of February 12, 1907, began like any other evening in Savannah as Patrolman J. N. Lewis made his usual rounds that took him to the old Union Station on West Broad Street shortly before midnight. He had been notified that his presence was needed to assist railroad authorities in apprehending an old gray mule that had appeared suddenly in the station about the time an inbound train had discharged its passengers at the gates.

It seems that a train had pulled into the station, and as debarking passengers were passing through a gate single file, a large whitish shape was noticed in the vicinity of the gates separating the train tracks from the Union Station doors. In front of the astonished passengers, who no doubt rubbed their eyes in an effort to give credence to the sight before them, the figure of an old gray mule materialized in full view of the passengers and workers there. Knowing that railroad regulations prohibited such intrusions as loose livestock wandering in and around the railroad gates, Union Station workers and officials, aided by some of the passengers, attempted to corral the animal, but to no avail. Their efforts caused the mule to panic, and it made a mad dash for the entrance that led inside the station. A comic scene unfolded as numerous parties pursued the frightened mule in a mad chase.

It was at this point that Patrolman Lewis arrived on the scene, and in what must have been a truly heroic endeavor, managed to capture the mule, thus preventing the animal from entering the Union Station waiting room. Leading the animal toward a call box in order to get assistance in removing the mule from the premises, the unthinkable happened. Before the very eyes of Patrolman Lewis, numerous passengers, and railroad personnel, the gray mule simply vanished! An immediate search of the area failed to produce a mule, or any other animal, for that matter.

There were those present among the spectators at this remarkable occurrence who recalled an older tradition of an elderly drayman who had recently passed on to his reward. This man had spent many years at his labors at the train depot. Perhaps, some conjectured, the deceased drayman had returned to the scene of his labors, in the form of a gray mule. No satisfactory explanation was ever recorded in the newspaper.

Certainly, passengers arriving or leaving Savannah by train that night witnessed an incident that would occupy their thoughts for some time to come. Eventually, after many whispered observations, explanations, and conversations, things at Union Station quieted down and things generally returned to normal. No doubt this strange appearance was the topic at many a gathering for days to come. Who could possibly forget the night Patrolman Lewis tried to arrest a ghost? It happened in Savannah!

Hogzilla Wasn't Hogwash!

While many Southerners, especially those of older generations, are known for their tall tales, sometimes it is hard to separate fact from fiction. The following account appeared in several newspapers in June of 2004 and stirred up much controversy as to verifiable facts in the case of the giant hog. In October of 2006, I spoke with Ken Holyoak who provided me with the following information on this world record hog.

The story begins in the little Georgia town of Alapaha, a quiet rural community located in Berrien County, which reported a population of 682 in the 2000 census. Like many small rural communities, a popular pastime, for the male portion of the population anyway, is hunting. Thus, in the spring of 2004 reports of a very large hog roaming River Oak Plantation generated enough interest among the hunting population of the county to the extent that the hog became the prime objective among hunters. Descriptions of the animal included 9-inch tushes and a body that was more than 12 feet long and weighed approximately half a ton. He was red in color, although other large hogs that had been spotted on the plantation were all black and white mixed.

In June of that year, a man by the name of Chris Griffin, an employee at River Oak Plantation, shot and killed the giant animal. Ken Holyoak, the owner of River Oak Plantation, was astounded when he saw the size of the hog. He was quoted in a newspaper as saying that the head of the animal was as big as a car tire. Since the hog was too large to be placed in a regular large freezer, and commercial meat lockers could not store the animal due to health regulations, and the size and age made the meat unsuitable for eating, the men who killed the beast decided to bury the animal. Mr. Holyoak had tried to have it stored in a cooler he had that had the capacity for twenty hogs, but his crew was not able to get the carcass through the door.

Mr. Holyoak took a few pictures of the hog, and several people who claimed to witness the shooting signed affidavits testifying to the size of the hog. Because there were rumors that there were some who might try to dig up the beast, Mr. Holyoak cut the head, which weighed 100 pounds, from the body, since that is where the tusks were located and he had not been able to accurately measure them. He buried the head some distance away from the body of the hog.

Many people in the area were not so sure of the reports of the size and weight of the hog, and some doubted that the hog even existed. This did not stop Alapaha from capitalizing on the story, however. In fact, "Hogzilla," as it was christened, put the little community of Alapaha on the map, bringing it instant fame. Thus, another urban legend was born. A short-lived fall festival, the Hogzilla Festival, was born. A life-sized replica of Hogzilla was created by a biologist working for Mr. Holyoak who based her replica on descriptions and measurements of the hog, and it became the mascot for the festival, appearing on a float during the festival parade.

Despite all of this, controversy over the existence of a Hogzilla continued to divide the town. Finally, in November of 2004, the National Geographic Channel sent a team of two forensic scientists and a camera crew to Alapaha with the express purpose of unearthing the remains of Hogzilla in order to confirm the stories that were circulating.

According to Holyoak, the two scientists projected a negative attitude as the digging commenced to exhume the hog. Since the animal had been buried extremely deep in the earth, the scientists began to comment among themselves that they did not believe there was a hog. When the remains were finally unearthed, the scientists measured the remains as they lay in the pit. Because the body had crumpled upon itself when dropped in the pit, the measurements taken were not accurate at all. When the head was dug up, the meat on the head had decomposed, revealing very long, thick tushes. In trying to remove the tushes from the skull, the scientists broke them, leaving a good two inches still in the skull. Once again, they were reluctant to give credence to the actual length, which would eventually prove to be about 18 to 20 inches for each.

At the conclusion of this examination, Hogzilla's remains were reburied in the original site.

The results of this undertaking by the investigators wearing their biohazard suits were interesting to say the least. Hogzilla was declared to be fact not fiction; the only dissenting votes concerned the actual size and weight. The forensic team determined that the weight of the monster pig was actually 800 pounds, and it was measured as being 8 feet in length. The large tushes were measured at 16 and 18 inches respectively. DNA testing showed some surprising results. Hogzilla had the DNA of a wild boar.

Ken Holyoak and Chris Griffin attributed the measurement differences to the shrinkage that had occurred during the time the boar was in the ground. He also said that he had measured Hogzilla at the beginning, and his measurements were of a hog that was 12 feet in length, 4 feet high, and 3 feet thick. He weighed out at 1,000 pounds. Taking into account the broken portion of the tushes would make the tushes 20 inches in length. Regardless of the apparent discrepancies in terms of weight and length, Hogzilla was still a whole lotta hog. Indeed, he was a world record.

River Oak Plantation is home to a very large fish hatchery, raising bream. Because the employees feed the fish every evening with a 45% protein-based fish food, the wild hogs in the area come down to the hatchery and go in the water to eat the fish food. Commercial hog farmers generally feed their hogs a food that is only about 14% protein. The difference in the amount of protein may contribute to the extraordinary growth of the wild hogs. According to Holyoak, they had once killed a 600-pound hog there. It is not unusual to see several large wild hogs in the vicinity.

The shooting of Hogzilla, and the subsequent publicity that arose when *National Geographic* decided to investigate the claims that a giant hog had been killed, unleashed a frenzy of publicity for the little town. Several television news stations, such as CNN, some as far away as Japan came to cover the event. Movie companies in California and in England expressed an interest in producing movies about this phenomenon. The various tabloids managed to include the story in their publications. Little did Holyoak and Griffin realize that by ridding the plantation of a monster hog they were literally writing the history of the little Berrien community. While the forensic scientists were bent on disproving the claims made regarding Hogzilla, in the end Holyoak and Griffin were vindicated. In retrospect, Mr. Holyoak says that he wished that he had leased a refrigerated truck to preserve the carcass. Although a taxidermist was present when the hog was killed, the estimated cost for mounting the animal, $10,000, seemed prohibitive at the time. Now, Mr. Holyoak says that had he assumed the cost of mounting the animal, he could have sold it for many times the cost of the taxidermy, but he had no idea that Hogzilla would turn out to be a world record. Alapaha, Georgia, enjoyed its moment of fame. Fame is fleeting, however, and in January of 2007, a hunter in Fayette County, Georgia, reported killing an 1100 pound pig. This event did not deter Lithium Productions who in May of 2007 issued a casting call for actors who would like a possible role in "The Legend of Hogzilla," a horror film produced by Rick Trimm, due to be filmed in June on location in little Alapaha, Georgia. Chris Griffin will be an advisor and consultant for the movie.

In the past year, reports of even more gigantic hogs being killed in Georgia made the major news networks. One report of a boar measuring more than eight feet long and weighing in excess of 1,000 pounds was killed by a young boy who tracked the animal and shot it. For a little while, the young hunter had his place in the sun until it was revealed that the hog was a domesticated, farm-raised animal whose owner stepped forward and burst the bubble of another massive wild boar roaming the Georgia woods. With all the competition, Hogzilla still claims the public attention. The upcoming movie may ring in a whole new era of horror stories. In the meantime, Alapaha modestly revels in the publicity.

Animal or Apparition?

Alapaha was not the only small Georgia town to be inhabited by an unusual beast. In 1955, the little rural town of Edison, Georgia, was traumatized by reports of a mysterious animal that was variously described in the newspapers as resembling either a kangaroo that fell in a barrel of flour, or perhaps, a werewolf, or possibly a ghost. Admittedly, these two creatures do not bear the slightest resemblance to each other, and it is difficult to understand how a kangaroo and a loup garou could be confused with each other. The description of this animal included claws for fingers, talons for toes, long, white shaggy hair, and the ability to leap six-foot high fences. A number of people claimed to have spotted this unusual animal, and perhaps this accounts for the conflicting descriptions.

According to an article written by James Sheppard for *The Albany Herald* on July 27, 1955, the initial sighting of the strange animal occurred near the small community of Parksville on the Three Springs Ranch. A 20-year-old black man by the name of Tant King supposedly saw the creature first. King was unable to provide the reporter with very much information, because in his own words he "didn't stay around long enough to observe many details." An elderly woman, who resided in the vicinity of the original sighting, claimed that she had seen it on several separate occasions over the past two years. Other reports of this mysterious creature stated that it was said to walk on its hind legs, leaving footprints that looked like those of a large dog. When one observer suggested that the creature was a ghost, more level-headed citizens scoffed and replied that other "spirits" were likely the explanation for the sightings. Other equally clear-headed citizens disputed this claim, and stated that they had also seen the thing.

One report stated that the owner of the farm where the creature was spotted indicated that he did not go walking around the farm at night. A friend of his discovered a hank of hair caught on a fence post over which the creature leaped. The hair was supposedly sent to the state crime laboratory in Atlanta for analysis, but the director of the crime laboratory had been tied up with a court case and had not had time to analyze the hair.

Despite the fear generated in the community, there were no reports of anyone being injured or property stolen or damaged. No evidence of foul play had been reported.

Oddly enough, another interesting item appeared in the *Atlanta Constitution* on July 26, 1955, that might possibly have some bearing on the reports. This article stated that on the afternoon of July 20, 1955, a farmhand in Edison, Georgia, observed a gray, four-foot tall, nude, hairy man walk out of the woods. This strange little man was visible for about 25 minutes as he walked along a fence. He then went back into the woods.

Were the two separate events related in any way? It seems more than coincidental that both occurred within the same week in the same farm community of Edison. Neither of the two separate events caused any real problems other than that of generating fear in the community. Reputable people such as the sheriff of Calhoun County, a vocational agriculture instructor, and the chief of police attested to the fact that something strange was happening in Edison. None of them offered any concrete opinion as to what this might be. The 1950s seem to have been a decade when numerous reports of U.F.O's, alien creatures, and other similar activities were being reported in communities across America. Perhaps the incidents in little Edison were part of a national trend.

Litchfield Plantation

The countryside surrounding much of Savannah is the location of a number of old plantations, many of which were deeded by crown grants to various individuals in the 1700s. The houses and other buildings are long gone for the most part, and memories of these old plantations live only in the names on rural road signs or on county maps. They speak of another era, and tell tales of love, heartbreak, and even, perhaps, murder.

Litchfield Plantation is one of these old tracts. Located to the south of Savannah city limits, the tract extends south to the delta of the Ogeechee River. The earliest mention of this site is found in old colonial records that list Joseph Wright as the petitioner for a grant to this acreage in August of 1760. There is some speculation among researchers that Wright was an Indian agent and interpreter for Governor Henry Ellis. This position would have been an extremely important one in colonial Georgia.

Few details are available about Joseph Wright, but it is known that he and his wife Mary Ann had two known children, a daughter, Mary Jane, born in 1780, and Joseph, Jr. There was possibly a third child as well. Speculation on the matter suggests that Joseph, Jr. and the elusive third child likely died young, for the elder Wright left all of his worldly possessions to Mary Jane. His will made no mention of any other surviving children

Mary Jane Wright married James Gunn in 1785, and with this union, the seeds of tragedy were sown. The marriage, in

137

accordance with the prevailing customs of that period, gave Mary Jane's new husband complete control and ownership of Mary Jane's wealth, including the title to Litchfield.

James Gunn was born in Virginia March 13, 1753. He was twenty-nine years old when he came from Virginia to the Savannah area in 1782. Having studied law and gaining admittance to the bar, he opened a practice in Savannah. He bought a lot in Savannah and two plantations, Clifton and Cashel Hall. He was an officer in the militia, having attained the rank of colonel during the Revolution. According to various reports, he possessed a hot temper and had acquired the reputation of being high-handed in his dealings with others. He also indulged in strong drink and was known for his drunken and riotous conduct. These attributes, along with his part in the Revolution, had earned him the sobriquet of "The Chatham Wasp." His temper led to a dispute with General Nathanael Greene involving an Army horse that Gunn had taken to replace the one he had lost in battle. Gunn then traded this new horse for another horse and two slaves. Greene had the matter brought before a court of inquiry. The court gave a verdict in Gunn's favor, thus enraging Greene who denounced the court and referred the matter to Congress. The Continental Congress ruled that officers had no right to sell Army property without authorization. When Greene took up residence at Mulberry Grove after the Revolution, James Gunn then challenged Greene to a duel. Greene ignored the challenge after being advised by his friend George Washington that "a commanding officer is not a free agent and few military decisions are not offensive to one party or the other."

James Gunn entered politics in Georgia through his military activities during the Revolution. He had risen from colonel of the Chatham County Militia and then to Brigadier General in the Georgia Militia. In 1787, Gunn was elected to the Continental Congress, although he never attended. When the Constitution was adopted in 1769, its provisions called for two senators from each state, and James Gunn and William Few were elected to fill these positions. This accorded Gunn the honor of being the first Senator from Georgia, a position he held for three terms. When Gunn's vote on approving Jay's Treaty with Great Britain in 1795 gave the Federalists a majority, a group met at the courthouse in Savannah and burned Jay in effigy and Gunn as well, proclaiming their acts treason. Gunn's role in the Yazoo Land fraud brought more criticism that was still being recounted after his death in Louisville, Georgia, the state capitol, in 1801.

James Gunn's marriage to Mary Jane Wright by all extant accounts was not a particularly happy one. There were no children born of this union, at least none that can be determined. Certainly, there were no children who lived to grow up. Mary Jane's maid revealed that the young Mrs. Gunn endured miseries, but did not relate the causes of these miseries. The maid stated that Mary Jane obtained a bottle of strong poison, which she kept close at hand. After Gunn returned from one of his business ventures, Mary Jane confined herself in her room, declaring that she would never share his bed again. When Gunn insisted on entering his wife's room, she, by all accounts, swallowed a strong dose of the poison. This gossipy tidbit was related in a letter written by Major General James Jackson on June 11, 1797, to Georgia Governor John Milledge. Jackson had received his information from females in his family who in turn had received the information from Mary Jane's maid. What transpired between Gunn and his wife behind the doors of her room, and what prompted such an illegal and sinful act that resulted in her untimely death? James Gunn was noted for his violent temper. Did he take an active part in his wife's demise? Records are silent on the matter, but Mary Jane's death did fuel much speculation on her relationship with her husband and on his character.

Mary Jane Wright Gunn died May 13, 1797, under mysterious circumstances, to say the least, and was buried in her family graveyard on Litchfield Plantation with her father. James Gunn did not remarry after the death of Mary Jane. The account of Gunn's death appeared in the *Georgia Gazette*, July 31, 1801. Like the death of Mary Jane, his death also raised some interesting questions. According to the published account, Brigadier General James Gunn died July 30, 1801, after a very short illness. The cause of death was attributed to his drinking cold water after taking some medicine. To further complicate matters, the doctor and several other men were in the room at the time, and no one noticed his death for quite some time. After Gunn's death, Litchfield went to a nephew, James Gunn of Richmond, Virginia. Although James Gunn was buried in Louisville, with military honors, it is very possible that his nephew James Gunn who inherited Litchfield lies in the Wright burial ground on the plantation.

Today, only one monument remains to mark any of the Wrights' graves. It is a table tomb that bears the following inscription on its surface:

In Memory of
JOSEPH WRIGHT
And his Daughter, Mary Jane

Departed this Life
the 22nd of June 1773
JOSEPH WRIGHT, Esqr.
Aged 45 Years and two Months

On the 13th of May 1797
Departed this Life
Mrs. MARY JANE GUNN
Aged 32 Years Six Months
And ten days.

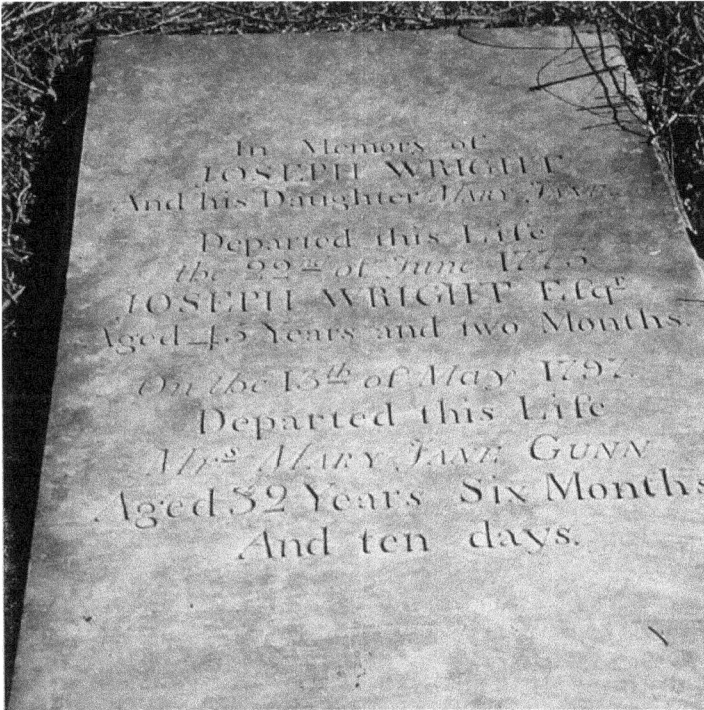

Debunking the Myths

Playing the devil's advocate is not an easy role, nor is it a popular role. Sometimes, however, an advocate is important in separating fact from fiction, or perhaps it would be more accurate to say fiction from fact. It is a fact that within the past ten years, Savannah has attracted a great many people who have not only resurrected old folk tales, but have been instrumental in giving Savannah the dubious distinction of "the most haunted city in America." This has been achieved by creating new tales of hauntings, until every building and street corner has been declared occupied by one or more spirits. It is really getting crowded here.

Some of the stories told have been around a long, long time. Unfortunately, far more are newcomers to our charming city, and they are related by people who frequently never heard of Savannah until they arrived here. Perhaps, the Spanish moss, with its eerie tendrils works on the imagination, as do the old buildings surrounding our squares, and the night fogs that occasionally drift in from the river. Even our cemeteries are not exempt from exploitation as tourists and actors try to recreate and photograph the dead rising from their graves. These are the dead who were given church burials and consigned to the grave to "Rest in Peace." Suddenly everyone is a ghost buster. Droplets of moisture from the air or reflections of lights show up on photographs and are declared "orbs" by the self-proclaimed experts. These "orbs" are supposed to be spirits. On occasion small mirrors have been attached to tombstones and reflect light when flash photos are taken from the outside of the iron fence. Voila! Instant orbs. No doubt some of the 'spirits' were once found only in bottles, but now come from 'go cups'.

Come on people! When you die, and discover that it is possible to return and visit the living, where would you hang out? There may be ghosts, but why on earth would a disembodied spirit hang around a graveyard? They would certainly seek a more interesting place to visit and haunt. What would be the point of flitting around a cemetery? Why would you want to appear in front of strangers? Surely, your relatives and loved ones would be a better choice to socialize with instead of a bunch of crappy tourists clicking their ubiquitous cameras while their guide tries to expound on what ghosts do or don't do.

Now, I know that strange things do happen, and many people through the ages have experienced unexplainable phenomena that smacks of the supernatural. There are many haunting stories that have been "authenticated" by virtue of their longevity.

Occasionally, a restless spirit might materialize to convey some message or to resolve some unfinished business. Usually these stories are not nearly as dramatic as ones we hear today. They are often simple stories and involve such elements as a door that mysteriously opens and closes by itself, a picture that falls off the wall for no discernible reason, or an apparition that appears at certain established times in predictable places to engage in repetitious behavior. Skepticism rears its head, however, when suddenly several different hotels or inns advertise a haunted room, and the haunted room number is designated as being room 204. That seems to be a popular number. The basic elements usually include a child who runs around the inn or a lady who roams around pulling the bedcovers off of the unwary. Savannah must have had a lot of children who played in hotel hallways and a lot of ladies who evidently found pulling covers off sleeping people a marvelous way to spend eternity.

One of the often-told tales, and an old one at that, is that of Captain Flint, a pirate who is said to haunt a certain establishment on East Broad Street. Robert Louis Stevenson passed through Savannah on his way to California in the late 1870s.

When he wrote *Treasure Island* in 1883, Stevenson had Captain Flint dying in Savannah, calling for Darby to "bring aft the rum." Research into Stevenson's life and into the world of pirates and buccaneers fails to produce a Captain Flint for the simple reason that he did not exist. The character of Captain Flint was created by Stevenson himself, who modeled his character on Captain England, a real pirate, and other notorious historical figures. To put it bluntly, there was no Captain Flint.

The Place that Captain Flint "haunts"

Another mythical spirit is that of Rene Rondolo Asch. There is no solid evidence that such a person existed in Savannah. No historical document in the history of Savannah mentions Rene, much less a family by the name of Asch or even Rondolo. No census from the early days lists the family, nor do early tax documents. The Ash family was a well-respected family in Savannah, and some members of that family lie in Colonial Cemetery. Of Rene, there is no mention in any document, yet knowing the style of journalism in the eighteenth and nineteenth centuries in Savannah, had such an unusual person existed and committed the atrocities attributed to Rene, it would have been reported in great detail in the newspapers. It would also have been recorded in the colonial records of Georgia.

It is more likely that Rene Asch was a story created to keep children in line. He was the booger man, and parents used the story to make children behave and stay indoors at night. Several generations of Savannahians grew up with the story of this giant of a man who strangled kittens and young ladies.

And then there is the account of someone renovating one of the old homes and finding the skeletal remains of a person hidden inside a wall. Some of these remains are frequently dressed in Confederate uniforms. None of these so-called "true" stories have ever been documented in Savannah. A story as sensational as this would have been meticulously dissected by the media and early newspapers were no exception. Such a story would have been too good to let pass unpublished. Have you ever considered how deep the walls of our homes would have to be to contain a human body? Then, too, there is the problem of unpleasant odors that would be very difficult to ignore.

Voodoo, the religion that was brought to these shores from Africa and from the Caribbean is another matter altogether. The practice of voodoo is a very real thing, and it was practiced in the South. In fact, it is still practiced today by some devotees. The practice of this religion, for that is what voodoo is, was quite common along the Atlantic coastline and the Gulf of Mexico. A version of voodoo, known as Santeria, is well-known in parts of Florida today.

That Gallant Polish Count

Few real figures in our country's history have stirred the imagination with such gallant deeds at the famed Count Casimir Pulaski. While not denigrating the efforts of the Marquis de LaFayette in the battle for American independence, it was Count Pulaski's daring feats that earned him a niche in America's hall of heroes. He became a martyr for American freedom.

Many excellent biographies have been written about Pulaski's life and I have no desire to intrude in an area that requires greater expertise than I possess. Rather, it is my intention to relate a portion of this man's life and death as it pertains to Savannah, particularly in the realm of legend. More specifically, an account of his burial, and his "resurrection" in the 1990s, is the topic of the following account.

Casimir Pulaski was born March 4, 1747, in the Masovia province of central Poland. At a very early age he mastered the equestrian skills that would serve him so well when he later entered the Polish military as a cavalryman. When barely nineteen, Pulaski joined his father Jozef and his brothers in organizing the Knights of the Holy Cross, a group determined to free Poland from Russian military occupation. The Knights took a solemn vow never to marry until Poland was free. Pulaski participated in a number of military engagements, but it was the last expedition that resulted in Pulaski's being falsely accused of a plot to assassinate the king. He was forced to leave his beloved Poland, never to return. In 1776, after learning of America's war for independence from England, he offered his services to the Americans. Upon a letter of recommendation from Benjamin Franklin, General George Washington, who was badly in need of seasoned officers, accepted Pulaski on his staff.

Few indeed are Georgians, especially those from Savannah, who have not learned of the gallant Count's efforts during the siege of Savannah in October of 1777. Fewer still are those who do not know that he was wounded in the thigh as he led a cavalry charge against the English forces. It is at this point however, that the accounts surrounding his demise become somewhat murky. Taken from the battlefield, the stricken Count was taken to the Bowen plantation known as Greenwich. There he was treated, but gangrene developed in the wound. He died October 11, 1777.

It is at this point that the accounts differ. According to one group, the dying Count was taken aboard the U.S.S. *Wasp*. The ship sailed for Charleston, South Carolina, but Casimir Pulaski died before reaching the port of Charleston and was buried at sea. For many years, this was the accepted story that appeared in the history books.

Meanwhile, back at Greenwich Plantation, a very different story began to circulate. This version told of the death of the County, and the subsequent burial of his remains by slaves under a giant oak tree on the plantation. This story was passed down through several generations of slaves who had been told the story by their forefathers who assisted in the clandestine burial so that the British would not desecrate the grave of this brave officer.

In 1850, a movement to honor the Polish count with a monument became a reality. Mr. Bowen, the owner of Greenwich Plantation, after to listening to some of his older slaves and their oral tradition of burying the Count beneath an oak, gathered some of his farmhands and had them dig on the site. Human remains were uncovered which were subsequently placed in a metal box. This box was then placed inside the monument in Monterey Square during the dedication ceremony.

In the 1990s, when the monument was declared a hazard to people walking through the square, the monument was dismantled for repairs. Inside the cornerstone was found the metal box, with its strange contents. Forensic examination by experts and DNA testing, using DNA material from a living relative in Poland, seemed to indicate that the remains were indeed those of the gallant Count. However, since none of the experts would commit themselves to an absolute certainty regarding the identity of the remains, it was decided to bury them in front of the monument with an uninscribed marble slab covering the grave. An elaborate ceremony was planned, with the remains inside a wooden coffin made in Poland, lying in state at all of the major churches in Savannah.

Bishop Ploski officiating at the burial of Count Pulaski

A procession from the Cathedral of St. John the Baptist, including Polish cavalry officers on white stallions, escorted the coffin down the streets of Savannah to Monterrey Square where it was placed in the grave. DNA material was saved, and when the day comes that technology can determine without a doubt that these remains are of Count Pulaski, and then the slab will be appropriately engraved.

A tragic footnote to this event, however, occurred April 10, 2010, when a plane carrying a number of Polish dignitaries crashed in Smolensk, Russia. Among the victims was Bishop Ploski who had been in Savannah for the burial of Count Pulaski.

Unrepentant Rebel

The War for Southern Independence, or War of Northern Aggression, as some call that terrible conflict that pitted brother against brother and ended after four long years with more casualties on both sides than all other wars fought by Americans combined, gave the South a rich legacy of heroism, courage, and bravery. The stories of the dedicated men – white, black, rich, poor, slave, and free – who fought to defend their homeland from an invasion that originated in the political parlors in Washington and culminated four years later at Appotamattox Courthouse in Virginia, serve as a reminder of what can happen when a government becomes too powerful and too self-serving to govern the country righteously. More misconceptions have been promoted regarding those terrible years, referred to by those of our elders who were not so far removed from that era as "The War." Today, our children do not know the full story, having cut their teeth on the version deemed most acceptable in public schools today. History is written by the victors and serves to justify any atrocities committed in the name of freedom.

Indeed, many school systems today tend to gloss over that period of our history as if it were of no consequence. Most early textbooks that recounted the history of the United States at that time were written by Northern historians who glorified their military and condemned those of the South as traitors. The turmoil created by the Battle Flag of the Confederacy, erroneously referred to as "The Stars and Bars" by the great host of the uninformed, serves to underscore the sort of sanitizing that is prevalent in our society today.

For the record, I would be remiss if I did not explain that the Confederacy had five flags, the first of which was the Stars and Bars, correctly identified as the First National Flag of the Confederacy. The Battle Flag with its St. Andrew's cross was originally used as a Confederate naval jack and was square. Today, that flag is condemned as being a symbol of racism, a false designation it has never deserved. Neither the Rebel Battle Flag, nor any other flag used by the Confederacy, ever flew on any slave ship, nor was it used by the Ku Klux Klan. It has been corrupted since the 1950s by various groups who desecrate it in ignorance because they do not know or understand its history. Brave, good men died under that banner, and that fact should never be forgotten. It had nothing to do with slavery, and everything to do with honor.

Aside from all the vagaries, misconceptions, and glossing over of facts and actual events, there were Southrons who held fast to their loyalties and beliefs and managed to carry on their lives as best they could under the circumstances without sacrificing the knowledge of their own self worth. Some of these rose to unequalled heights of glory, and in spite of attempts to discredit them, are as well known today as one's own family members.

Others, just ordinary people, performed their duties quietly and without fanfare. They performed the tasks set before them and carried out their duties without complaint. Their stories live only in the family circles that refuse to let those loyal souls drift away into obscurity. This is the heart of the real South, the one that never succumbed to the idea of their cause being lost.

Earlier generations of children heard these simple stories when the family gathered round a supper table or a fireplace after the evening meal. This was truly a family time, and few indeed were families that did not spend at least sometime together after supper. Television was still in its infancy, and organized sports for young people that required evening attendance were unheard of.

It was at such times that old stories and anecdotes were recalled, and children sat spellbound as their elders spoke of a time in the past when people struggled to make sense of a world gone mad. Certainly, the children seemed to relish hearing these stories repeated many times. The fascination of another era held them captive. It was here that one's heritage was preserved and remembered.

The percentage of families that eat an evening meal together, and then sit around and reminisce about their family's past is quite small today. Modern young people have been indoctrinated into the media hype that such knowledge has no relevance in these hectic and technologic times. Many of the younger generation have no idea of who they are or where they came from. The here and now is all that matters, and values of the past have no place in modern lives.

Nevertheless, these things are relevant, and they do have immense value. Certainly, a century ago no young person was compelled to find himself. He already knew who he was and where he was going. There was no compulsion to belong, because he already belonged to a family whose values took precedent over those of his friends. He also belonged to his community. If there were uncertainties, he had his vast family history and tradition upon which to build.

Unfortunately, for not only the South, but also for people in other parts of the country who were once distinguished by their individuality and culture, today's media has infiltrated every facet of our lives, even our speech patterns are changing rapidly as young people buy into the hype that Southern accents sound as if one is illiterate and therefore such accents are undesirable.

Quickly vanishing are the old tidewater vowels of Virginia, Charleston, Wilmington, and Savannah's "Geechee" softness that falls on the ear with the gentleness of a magnolia petal floating on a summer breeze. Vanishing also is the soft melodical speech of the Lumbee, the near Cockney tones of the Outer Banks of North Carolina, the twang of the Southern highlands, with its hint of Gaelic brogue and the lyrical cadences of the Creole and the Cajun. Those soft Southern voices are disappearing, being replaced by the loudness and harshness of New York, Chicago, and Hollywood. We are rapidly losing our individuality and our uniqueness that makes our homeland so desirable to outsiders. We are literally selling our birthright to become lemmings, blindly running after some invisible target. To our detriment, we have become a mass society. Even the word "lady" has fallen into disuse in many places.

Some of the following stories reflect the type of stories a child growing up in the early part of the twentieth century might hear at the family table. While seemingly inconsequential, they were often instrumental in the overall development of the child fortunate enough to hear them, because most instilled old-fashioned values of loyalty, honesty, friendship, and most of all, family.

Southern Belles

Southern ladies, of necessity, have had to overcome seemingly insurmountable odds to achieve their goals. This quality has shaped the course of Southern history in a quieter way than that of their male counterparts. Nevertheless, their contributions were of incalculable value. Some of these ladies were years ahead of their time in what they were able to accomplish. Some made their mark in less obtrusive ways. Whatever the means by which they made their mark, whatever the magnitude of their contributions, each was important to the time in which they lived. It is that context that is important, for that is how they are remembered.

This section focuses on several women that I felt should be raised up from their relative anonymity and recognized for the things they accomplished in what was essentially a man's world during the period in which they lived. None of them ever was included in the history books that describe the achievements of our ancestors. Certainly, their lives did not change the history of their country in any major way. None of them ever held a political office, nor did they attain celebrity status, although a few may have been associated with some historically important figures. The ladies I chose to discuss in this section all had one thing in common. By some quirk of fate, all of them were named Mary. One was likely the first medical doctor in Georgia; one was an astute businesswoman and entrepreneur without equal; and one, by one of those mysterious quirks of fate paired her with one of Dixie's most famous historical figures. There were other Mary's who had a significant impact on the history of Georgia. They include Mary Telfair, and Mary Musgrove, who acted as an interpreter for General Oglethorpe in his communications with the Yamacraw Indians.

Mary Lavinder

Mary Lavinder, the daughter of Benjamin and Rebecca Lavinder, was born October 18, 1778 on her father's plantation on Burnside Island in Chatham County, Georgia. From all available accounts Miss Lavinder was a strong-willed individual, and it is likely that this stubborn trait appeared very early in her life. Certainly, it would shape her life.

Despite her family's efforts to train her for a role as mistress of a plantation, concentrating on the feminine pursuits which the majority of eighteenth century ladies indulged, Mary Lavinder apparently had other ideas as to what she intended to do with her life. She had developed an interest in medicine at a period in which this was not particularly accepted. Choosing to remain a spinster, sometime in the early 1800s, young Mary Lavinder began her career as a midwife.

For the daughter of a well-to-do plantation owner, this choice no doubt engendered numerous "discussions" within the confines of the Lavinder family. This career choice was clearly not in their plans for their rebellious daughter. But, being strong-willed and apparently well-versed in the art of persuasion, Mary Lavinder left Savannah and went to Philadelphia to study obstetrics as a private student of Professor Thomas E. James at the University of Pennsylvania Medical School.

Completing her studies with Professor James, Mary returned to Savannah about 1815 and set up an office and home on East York Street. There Miss Lavinder began treating children and women, these being the specialties she had trained for. Although Mary Lavinder had earned the right to be called "Doctor," this title was seldom used, especially for a female, and thus she was generally known as "Miss" Lavinder. In fact, this was her preference in order to avoid dissension among the male physicians in Savannah. In 1818, Miss Lavinder's reputation was such that two prominent obstetricians asked her to come to Boston to take over their practice. She turned down this offer, choosing instead to remain in Savannah.

By 1820, Mary Lavinder had a thriving practice in Savannah. Three devastating calamities befell Savannah in that year, all of which had a severe impact on the population of Savannah. During this bleak time, Miss Lavinder rendered medical care to those suffering from the yellow fever epidemic that plagued Savannah after a fire that had destroyed much of the city. The hurricane that hit in the aftermath of the fire resulted in many injuries as well. In all of these disasters, Miss Lavinder not only offered her medical expertise, but also spent much of her large income to provide for the poor victims of these disasters. She brought much needed supplies to those who had lost their homes to the fire that swept Savannah or to the hurricane that later drenched the burned-out Savannah. When yellow fever reared its ugly head later that same year, Miss Lavinder was there once again, offering comfort and medical care to those suffering from the dread fever.

Considered somewhat of an eccentric personality, Miss Lavinder was known for her generosity and charity. She cared little for personal comfort and despised the trappings of finery with which women of that day dressed. An article written by Dr. Victor H. Bassett who was librarian of the Georgia Medical Society in the 1930s, described Mary Lavinder as being a "plain lover of hard common sense and truth for its own sake." She was blunt and outspoken, and of a rather forbidding appearance. She was frequently seen traveling the streets of Savannah in her "chair," a low-slung carriage drawn by an old white horse, as she ministered to the sick and the poor, bringing with her coffee, sugar, tea, grits, and even blankets and mattresses. An extremely tolerant person, she was non-judgmental when confronted with the follies of her patients.

Mary Lavinder died November 19, 1845, in the old city she had served so long and faithfully. She was quite likely the first female medical doctor in Georgia. This claim was challenged a descendant of Dr. Palatia "Polly" Wilson Stewart who was born April 2, 1805 in Jones County, Georgia. Polly Wilson married Thomas Ware Stewart in 1821. She was sixteen years old at the time, and her family was very much opposed to the marriage. The Stewarts had thirteen children, six of whom were sons and served in the Confederate Army. Thomas Stewart died, leaving Polly the mistress of a large plantation with fifty slaves. In order to take care of the slaves, Polly studied medicine, and in May of 1848, she passed medical examinations and was given a diploma in medicine by The Botanico Medical Society of Hartford, Connecticut. During the War Between the States, Polly served the wounded and sick in the surrounding counties, including some of the Federal soldiers. Dr. Polly Stewart died July 11, 1866.

If one compares the significant dates of Mary Lavinder with those of Polly Stewart, it appears that Mary Lavinder, who had formal medical training, was practicing medicine before Polly Stewart came on the scene.

Mary Leaver Marshall

The only child of Gabriel and Mary Schick Leaver, Mary Magdalen Leaver, was born in Savannah in 1783. Gabriel Leaver was a prominent Savannah cabinetmaker that had come from England. His wife, Mary Schick was very distantly related to Peter Tondee's family by marriage. Gabriel was an astute businessman who invested in property on Broughton Street and elsewhere throughout the city. When Leaver died, October, 23, 1795, he left his entire fortune, which consisted of several pieces of prime real estate and money, to his only child, Mary Magdalen Leaver.

On October 30, 1800, at the age of 16, young Mary Leaver

married a Savannah banker named James Marshall. No children were born to the couple, but Mary Marshall, evidently well-taught by her father and no doubt by her banker husband as well, took the legacy left to her by her father and continued his practice of buying properties throughout the city. She purchased livery stables, apartment or row houses, and inns, thereby amassing a substantial fortune of her own.

Portrait of Mary Leaver Marshall

Although Mary and James remained childless throughout her married life, in 1840, at the age of 56, Mary adopted Margaret, a young Irish immigrant. James Marshall died May 26, 1845, at the age of 64. It seems likely that Mary undertook the education of her adopted daughter. Margaret Marshall married Adelaut Barclay, the son of the British consul at New York in November of 1855. She and her husband had a daughter in 1858 whom they named Mary Marshall Barclay. Their marriage did not last, and in 1860 Margaret obtained a divorce from Barclay. Six years later, Margaret died, leaving her eight-year-old daughter Mary. Her grandmother, Mary, who was then 80 years old raised the child. When Mary Marshall died in 1877 at the age of 91, her wealth totaled more than $200,000 in bank assets, and also forty different properties which consisted of houses, stores, stables, the Marshall Hotel, built in 1851, and Marshall Row on East Oglethorpe Avenue. Her granddaughter, Mary Marshall Barclay, then 19 years of age, was her sole heir.

Today, Mary Marshall's grave is located in Laurel Grove Cemetery North.

Mary Ahearn

The story of Mary Ahearn was told to me by one of her collateral descendants who felt that her story had merit and was worthy of being shared. Hers is a story of loyalty and devotion to her employer who obviously considered her a part of his distinguished family. In order to understand her character it is necessary to first look at the background of events that would bring her and her family to a small, but important role in the history of the South. It is a simple story that should not be lost. It is typical of the family stories repeated at night as children and elders gathered round a fireplace or a table and spoke of their ancestors. I have narrated this story in the words of Paul F. Jurgenson, a prominent Savannah physician who told me the story of his great aunt, Mary Ahearn. It is as much his story as it is Mary's.

Ireland, in the early part of the 19th century, was a country in great turmoil. Political unrest and abuse, strict and unfair English penal laws, which were anti-Catholic, prevented many Irish from leaving the county. In the years 1830 and 1835, Ireland, under Dan O'Connell repealed the penal laws that had been in effect since 1690. These laws had deprived the

Catholics of their lands, and absentee English landlords, and the impending failure of the potato crop forced many to leave the auld sod and seek a better life in America.

One of these immigrants was Michael Ahearn, who along with his wife Bridget and daughter Mary settled in Eldora, a small rural community on the outskirts of Blitchton. The family was devout Catholic, and was no doubt the topic of speculation in that rural, predominantly Protestant setting about 25 miles from Savannah. Their farmhouse was located near the Bulloch County line at Black Creek.

Young Mary, who had been born in Ireland about 1835, probably grew up in that community, helping with farm chores and tending to the younger children in the family, for besides Mary herself, there were Ellen, James, Margaret, William, Michael, and later Sally, all of whom were younger and were all born in Georgia.

Eventually, Sally would enter the Catholic order of the Sisters of Mercy and help to establish St. Joseph' s Hospitals in both Savannah and in Atlanta. Margaret (or Meg as she was called) Ahearn would marry Timothy Quinn, a grocer in Savannah.

When the War Between the States came, the Ahearns, like their neighbors, cast their lot with the South. Many of the young Irish immigrants or the first generation Irish boys and girls went to work in the arsenal in Savannah.

In 1865, after the arrest of Confederate President Jefferson Davis, at Irwinville, his wife Varina Davis was sent with her children to Savannah. Because Jefferson Davis had been educated by Catholic orders in Kentucky, Varina enrolled her older children in St. Vincent's Academy in Savannah.

The Sisters of Mercy helped Mrs. Davis find a house on the northeast corner of Taylor and Bull streets. The younger Davis children were in need of a governess, as their old governess had stayed behind in Richmond. The kindly Sisters arranged for Mary Ahearn, who was then in her late twenties and unmarried, to become a governess to the younger Davis children. Varina Ann Davis, known to the family as Winnie, was two years old at the time.

The arrangement suited Mary Ahearn very well, and evidently, Mrs. Davis was well satisfied with the new governess, for Mary stayed with the Davis family for twelve years, from 1864 until 1877. She soon became much more than an employee, and traveled with the Davis family to Europe and Canada.

When General Sherman made his famous "March to the Sea' in 1864, he made a stop at the Ahearn farmhouse at Black Creek. At that time, the house was being used as a hospital for Federal troops. When the Federal troops finally left and pressed on to Savannah, they burned the house to the ground. Varina Davis, in a letter to her husband mentioned Mary and told of the burning of the Ahearn farmhouse by Union troops.

Jefferson Davis died in 1889 at the age of 81. He did not forget the devoted Irish girl who had cared for his children, and who had become an integral part of the Davis family. He bequeathed a roll top desk and a portrait of himself to Mary Ahearn. These two items were placed in the Ahearn house that had been rebuilt after the Federal troops had finally left the area for good.

Unfortunately, this second Ahearn house was also destroyed by fire. The roll top desk and the portrait of Jefferson Davis, which had been bequeathed to Mary, were consumed in this conflagration.

When Varina Davis died in 1906 in New York, she left Mary some jewelry and nearly $1,000 in cash. Mary, who never married, chose to remain with Winnie Davis as a companion. When Winnie died, she left Mary a portrait of herself, as well as a sum of money.

Mary herself died in June 5, 1914 at age 79. She was buried in Catholic Cemetery in Savannah in the same lot as some of her kinfolk. The portrait of Winnie Davis, the

Daughter of the Confederacy, was eventually passed down to William Barrett, a bachelor cousin of Mary's. Mr. Barrett gave the Winnie Davis portrait, which is a profile of Winnie, to the Savannah Chapter 2 of the United Daughters of the Confederacy. It remains a treasured relic in the archives of Savannah Chapter 2 to this day.

Grave of Mary Ahearn

Silk Dress Balloons

From the early 1700s and perhaps even earlier, according to some experts who even suggest that the line drawings on the Nazca Plain in Peru were accomplished through the use of balloons, men have been drawn to the idea of flight. Balloons made this idea an early reality, even though the methods of achieving this were rather crude and elementary. Exhibitions of such flights were occurring in several areas of Europe, and naturally spread to America. By the 1840s, a number of both tethered and untethered balloon ascensions were taking place in this country.

In 1860, a man by the name of Charles Cevor arrived in Savannah and brought with him a balloon that he may have purchased from John Wise, an early American pioneer in ballooning. In February of that same year, Professor Cevor, as he called himself, launched an exhibition of the "Montpelier" at the Armory Hall in Savannah. On March 9, 1860, Cevor, along with T. L. Dalton, who was the superintendent at Grover & Maker's Sewing Machines at I. W. Morrell & Co. in Savannah, ascended from Armory Hall in the "Montpelier." From the outset, things began to go wrong with the ascension. The balloon rose more than 10,000 feet in the air was caught in the lower portion of the jet stream, which whisked the balloon out over the Atlantic and Calibogue Sound. Cevor and Dalton were helpless, and they almost drowned when the control car of the balloon dragged through the water of the sound. At some point in the flight, both men were dumped out of the car and became stranded in the marshes near Hilton Head. A slave from a nearby plantation spotted the two men and rescued them from the marsh. The "Montpelier" had evidently continued its erratic flight without them and it was assumed lost. Professor Cevor and Mr. Dalton caught a steamer and returned to Savannah on March 12th. The Savannah Daily Morning News reported in its March 19th edition that the abandoned balloon was rumored to have been found near the Suwanee River in Florida.

Evidently, these mishaps, as well as public interest in such events, spurred the citizens of Savannah to offer Cevor some recompense for his loss, for in April of 1860, Cevor a letter to the editor of the Daily News in which he thanked the people of Savannah for collecting money to build a new balloon to replace the lost "Montpelier." He began constructing the replacement balloon in a storeroom on the Bay and named the new balloon "Forest City," a nickname then used for Savannah. On June 21, 1860, Cevor announced that the "Forest City" would make exhibition ascensions from the Barracks yard. Admission for the event was Fifty Cents. Another ascension was scheduled for Christmas Day, but due to bad weather, this was postponed until December 28. That ascension was witnessed by a large crowd. The "Forest City" ascended from the Chatham Academy yard on South Broad Street and traveled in a westerly direction. Savannahians later learned that Cevor landed safely on the other side of the canal and returned to the city that afternoon.

Charles Cevor obtained a job as an engineer at the Central of Georgia Railroad until the war clouds brewing over the country became a reality. In January of 1861 when the call went out for men to join the Confederate Army, Cevor enlisted in the First Georgia Infantry with the Chatham Artillery. He first served with Wheaton's Company, and later in Claghorn's Company.

Records regarding Cevor's Confederate service are sparse, but in 1862, General P.T.G. Beauregard requested that a balloon corps be formed for reconnaissance duty. Captain Langdon Cheves, a native Savannahian who had moved to South Carolina, came to Savannah in the spring of 1862 and set about constructing a balloon. Materials for many ventures were becoming scarce in the South, as the Union navy had blockaded many ports. The suggestion was made that if Southern ladies would donate their silk dresses, the material could be used to make a balloon. This statement, propagated by former General James Longstreet, gave rise to the charming legend that the ladies of the South immediately pulled out their silk dresses and gave them to the Confederacy for that purpose. While this story adds its romance to those legends of the so-called "Lost Cause," it was not exactly true.

In actuality, Cheves had ordered the purchase of 40-foot lengths of dress silk, which arrived in a multitude of colors and patterns. The silk lengths were sewn together and coated with a varnish made from old rubber car springs dissolved in oil to render the completed balloon gas tight. Charles Cevor, who by this time had attained the rank of Captain, supervised the construction of the balloon in Savannah. It was inflated with city gas. Tragedy struck however, on May 31, 1862. Two Irish men, William Harper and Martin Brennan, were on detached service from their military units and were stationed at the Savannah gashouse. Harper and Brannan were both overcome by the gas used to inflate the balloon and both men died. William Harper is buried in Laurel Grove Cemetery. His comrade, Martin Brennan was buried in Catholic Cemetery.

Despite the fatal accident, the colorful balloon, believed to have been named the *Gazelle*, was finally completed, shipped by railroad to Richmond, and saw its first service on June 27, 1862, at the battle of Gaines Mill. Confederate General Porter Alexander ascended in the balloon with another man, believed to be Cevor who was experienced in piloting the balloon. The reconnoitering expedition was apparently successful, and when the movement of Union troops finally took them out of range near Malvern Hill due to a weakening of the gas in the balloon, Alexander had it refilled and placed aboard the CSS *Teaser*, an armed tugboat, and took it down the James River. On July 4, 1862, the *Teaser* ran aground on a mud bank, and while its crew was working to free it, the Federal gunboat *Maratanza* appeared, forcing the crew to run into the woods to escape. The *Teaser* was captured along with the balloon. General Alexander escaped and made his way to Richmond to report the loss of the balloon to General Lee.

This was not the end of the military use of balloons by the Confederacy, however. Cevor evidently returned to Savannah during the summer of 1862 and set about the construction of another silk balloon. This balloon was completed and entered Confederate service. This second "silk dress" balloon was used until the summer of 1863 when it was lost at the siege of Charleston.

After the war, Cevor returned to Savannah and put on several exhibitions of his famed *Sterescoptican* at St. Andrews Hall in May of 1866. This exhibit was a benevolent undertaking with some of the proceeds going to the Savannah Widow's Society and some to the Union Society.

In 1868, Cevor was listed in Savannah's Roll of Honor as being a member of the Chatham Artillery during the war. There was a note that he was a resident of Valdosta in that year. Nothing further is known about Cevor. He seems to have been somewhat of a mystery man. Of his death, there is no record, but Georgia has not totally consigned him to obscurity.

While the Union Army did have a balloon corps, civilians staffed it. Captain Charles Cevor, C.S.A., was the first commissioned officer to use balloons for military purposes. As such, on April 29, 2006, Captain Charles Cevor and General Edward Porter Alexander of Augusta were honored by being inducted into the Aeronautical Museum at Warner Robins, Georgia.

The Ladies Gunboat Society

The war that forever changed the face of old Dixie took a terrible toll on the brightest and best of her sons. But that war was not the sole province of men. If anything, its impact on the women of the South was even more far reaching in many respects. Ladies who had previously been spared from actual physical labor now found themselves not only tending to their usual duties as mistresses of the rural plantations, but also involving themselves more intensely in pursuits that were once primarily the realm of their men folk. This was especially true in the financial world, particularly that of fundraising in order to procure much needed weapons and armaments. Women are often extremely creative when the necessity for obtaining funds for a worthy cause arises.

In 1861, the naval battle between the USS *Monitor* and the CSS *Virginia* (which had been refitted from the hull of the Merrimac) at Hampton Roads, Virginia, underscored the advantages of ironclads, a resource sorely lacking in the South, but one which had already proved its value. The Confederates eventually sank the CSS *Virginia* in 1862 in order to prevent its capture by Union naval forces. Various sources estimate the cost of building an ironclad at approximately $80,000, an exorbitant amount in the 1860s.

This sum did not deter the ladies, however, and groups were organized to raise money to build ironclad vessels for the South. While these groups of ladies were more formally organized in the port cities of the South, ladies from all over the South sent in contributions. It appears that the first such group of ladies, who reportedly were incensed by the capture of Port Royal by Federal troops, organized in New Orleans for the purpose of raising money for a gunboat. Other similar groups in Virginia, South Carolina, and in Georgia responded to appeals published in newspapers.

The methods employed by these determined and loyal Southern women took many different forms, but the end result was an astonishing sum of money for this endeavor.

Alabama ladies made quilts, which were then auctioned off, sometimes more than once, to raise the necessary money to purchase gunboats for the Confederacy. Indeed, a fierce competition arose among the Southern women to see which group could raise the most money. Gunboat Fairs were held in numerous cities to raise money. Some ladies throughout Georgia pledged various amounts, which were then totaled and forwarded to Savannah.

The Weekly Columbus Enquirer of March 18, 1862, sent an appeal to the editor of the *Macon Telegraph*, in which it was stated that a young lady in Summerville, South Carolina, had initiated a subscription to build a gunboat at Charleston. The letter went on to state that the writer was certain that there was enough patriotism among the ladies in Georgia to raise necessary funds to build a gunboat for "war-worn veteran Commodore Tattnall."

The Savannah Ladies Gunboat Association did not shirk their responsibilities either. They held their own gunboat fairs at which baked goods, jewelry, and bric-a-brac were sold, as well as securing "subscriptions," or donations as we would refer to them today. Where there is a will there is a way, and thus, together with monies sent from all over Georgia, the Association managed to raise more than $115,000. Black Confederates provided significant support for the gunboat associations as well. One free black man, in Columbus, Georgia, contributed $300 toward the building of the gunboat that became the CSS *Georgia*, an ironclad warship that would be put in service to defend Savannah's waterways. The proud CSS *Georgia* was built in Savannah and launched May 19, 1862, and had the distinction of being Georgia's first ironclad. Her armor was composed of 500 tons of railroad iron, and she boasted armament consisting of four Columbiads.

The CSS *Georgia* did not get to fulfill the hopes that she would go into an active role in defense of Savannah. Her propulsion system was not up to the task of maneuvering it in the tidal waters of the Savannah River. Instead, she became a floating battery in the waters in front of Old Fort Jackson. Sadly, the massive old ironclad came to an ignominious end. She was scuttled December 20, 1864, in order to keep her out of the hands of the Union troops that were approaching Savannah.

In 1866, Federal officers tried to dynamite the *Georgia* in order to clear the Savannah harbor of the wreckage and to salvage the iron. These efforts were not successful. The Army Corps of Engineers considered a second attempt in 1871, but the final consensus was that the proposal was too expensive.

Today, the pride of the Savannah Ladies Gunboat Association rests in about forty feet of water in the Savannah River, within a stone's throw of Fort Jackson. Archaeological explorations and dives have retrieved numerous artifacts, some of which are displayed at the old fort. Although there have been recent dives that have brought up more pieces of the *Georgia*, by and large she has been left alone. Perhaps one day the technical knowledge and adequate funding will combine to raise the *Georgia*. Until then, the Savannah Ladies Gunboat rests quietly in her watery grave.

A Steel Magnolia

The War Between the States gave rise to a number of women in the South who made their mark in the history of the South despite a male-dominated society. These delicate magnolias with steely reserve made decisions and embarked on courses that forever earned them a place in the history of the South.

One such lady was Miss Mattie Harris Lyons, born in 1850, whose unwavering determination to insure that the Confederate dead should not be forgotten in death resulted in the establishment of the Confederate Cemetery in Marietta, Georgia. This cemetery, established in 1863, by contains the remains of more than 3,000 Confederates, each with a stone to honor these men. There is also a monument to the Unknown Confederate Dead.

The land was owned by John Glover, the first mayor of Marietta, who had purchased a large parcel of land in 1848 when he arrived in what would become Marietta. Glover's wife, Jane, a member of the Memorial Association, donated the land in 1867, but the city had begun burying Confederate dead there in 1863. Many of the early Confederate burials came from area hospitals, and also men who died in an especially severe train wreck. Confederate Casualties from the battle at Kennesaw Mountain and Kolb's Farm also lie here. This practice was halted when General William T. Sherman captured the town.

When the War ended a man by the name of Henry Cole, a native of New York and the owner of a hotel in Marietta, donated land across town to be used as a cemetery for soldiers from both sides. Cole was soon exposed as a Yankee spy who had provided lodging in his hotel for Andrews' Raiders the night before they hijacked a train and precipitated "The Great Locomotive Chase."

The cemetery on Henry Cole's property soon became the burial site of thousands of Union dead who were brought from the battlefields of northwest Georgia, and it was not long before it was officially established as the Marietta National Cemetery.

The federal government was diligent in maintaining the Marietta National Cemetery.

Needless to say, the good citizens of Marietta had no desire to bury the honored Confederate dead next to those of Union soldiers. They continued to use the Confederate burial ground located on land donated by Glover. The Confederate Cemetery holds the remains of more than 3,000 Confederate soldiers who died at Chickamauga and at Ringgold. Many of these were unknowns and represented every Confederate state. In later years, Confederate Veterans who died at the Confederate Veterans' Home in Atlanta were brought here for interment.

However, the Confederate cemetery became overgrown and unkempt, as the state of Georgia found itself sorely lacking in funds to maintain the cemetery. By the early 1920s, the cemetery was in terrible condition, with bones of the dead often exposed along the road beside the cemetery.

It was at this point that the head of the Ladies Memorial Foundation, Miss Mattie Lyon, persuaded the State of Georgia to erect a fence around the burial ground and to mark the graves with stones. Her efforts were successful and neat rows of headstones were erected. Miss Mattie, as she was known, had a vested interest in this project.

Two of her stepbrothers never came home from the War. One of these was Captain Samuel Young Harris, who was wounded and captured at Sailors Creek in 1865 and died of his wounds in Virginia a few days later. Harris was killed by a stray round the day after the surrender. He was buried in a small Confederate Cemetery in Burkeville, Virginia. Perhaps Miss Mattie felt that by tending to the Confederate dead in her own hometown, someone would also care for her brothers' graves.

The Ladies Memorial Foundation had plans for the burial ground to become a garden created in the memory of the men buried there. One of the four cannon from the old Georgia Military Academy near Marietta was placed in the cemetery. This cannon had been captured by General Sherman and held as a war trophy. It was returned in 1910.

It soon became evident that plans envisioned for the Confederate Cemetery would not be realized due to the Ladies Memorial Foundation's inability to raise the money necessary for the task.

Miss Mattie died in 1947 at the age of 97. During her long life, she made her mark in a number of different endeavors. She was president of the Kennesaw Chapter of the United Daughters of the Confederacy®. She authored a book, *My Recollections of the War Between the States*, which was published in 1929. She was also credited with a major role in forming the first chapter of the American Red Cross in Marietta.

In 2004, a newly formed organization named the Confederate Cemetery Foundation decided to pay tribute to the lady who was the major figure in efforts to preserve this cemetery.

A bronze statue, designed by T.J Dixon, a contemporary sculptor of some renown, was erected at the gravesite of Miss Mattie Harris Lyon. It depicts Miss Mattie, sitting on a bench with an open book in her lap. She gazes out toward the Confederate burials, keeping vigilance over her "garden of heroes."

The Grave of Miss Mattie Harris Lyons

The Grave at Brampton Plantation

On the banks of the Savannah River, just a few miles from downtown Savannah, an ancient brick-walled family graveyard sits isolated from the bustle of everyday activities. A nearby industry goes about its daily routines without much thought for the history of its location.

Brampton Plantation was acquired by Jonathan Bryan in 1765. Bryan, a planter from South Carolina, owned several large pieces of property in and around Savannah. Brampton was also the home of Andrew Bryan, a slave who was educated and ordained a minister by Jonathan Bryan. Andrew Bryan was the founder of the First African Baptist Church in Savannah, and his likeness is the subject of one of the stained glass windows in that structure. The portion of Brampton's history that deals with the 1860s era is the part that is of special interest to me because of a discovery I made in the cemetery a few years ago that resulted in a lengthy search in libraries, museums, and local histories.

In the summer of 2002, Allison and Hannah Thurlow and I had spent much of a day driving around Chatham County looking for old graveyards to photograph and list. This was a personal project that fascinated us. Having come from the western part of the county, we were headed back into the city on Brampton Road. I mentioned that the old Brampton cemetery was somewhere in the vicinity, having seen old photographs that showed a brick crypt and wall. Supposedly, it was located near the National Gypsum plant.

We drove up to the plant office to ask directions, and

174

spoke with the office manager who agreed to take us to the cemetery that was located behind the plant. At some time or other, an unknown individual had placed a steel ladder or stile over the wall of the cemetery, there being no means of egress as there was no gate. We scrambled up and over the stile and entered the small graveyard. Only a few graves had stones, but one was marked as being that of Annie, a family servant. Most of the other stones were illegible, but one upright headstone caught my eye. The inscription stated that this was the grave of Major John C. Booth, C.S.A. who was born in 1827 in Macon, Georgia, and who died in Fayetteville, North Carolina, in September of 1862.

Grave of Major John C. Booth, CSA

Why was a Confederate soldier buried here in a graveyard that contained only graves dating from the late 1700s and very early 1800s? Major Booth's grave was apparently the last burial in this place.

The plant manager, who had accompanied us, could not provide any information on this burial. His behavior was somewhat odd as he talked about some employees who had once dug for bottles and other artifacts in this vicinity. He mentioned that once an employee found some old silver goblets and gave them to him. Warning bells chimed softly as he told us this, but he was not willing to offer more information. He did say that if we uncovered more information about the area, particularly the location of the old plantation house, he would be glad to share some information with us. We left the site with many unanswered questions, and the impression that we perhaps already knew more than we expected to learn. That plant manager has since moved on.

A trip to the Georgia Historical Society produced additional information about Brampton Plantation and Jonathan Bryan, including the fact that Sherman's troops, on their way north out of Savannah, pillaged and burned the plantation house, which at that period of time was owned by John Williamson. Of Major Booth, there was no information other than the fact that he was an early graduate of the Military Academy at West Point. Nothing indicated a reason for his presence at Brampton, especially in light of the fact that he had died in Fayetteville, North Carolina.

I spent much of the rest of that summer in Laurinburg, North Carolina. One morning I opened the morning newspaper, the *Fayetteville Observer*, and noted that someone had written an article on the Fayetteville Arsenal. This military installation was under the command of a small detachment of U.S. Army when North Carolina seceded from the Union in 1861. Governor Ellis ordered the North Carolina militia to seize the arsenal. Lieutenant DeLagnel, then commandant of the arsenal, surrendered without a shot being fired and the Fayetteville Arsenal became an important factor to the Confederate Army. Lieutenant DeLagnel resigned his commission in the U. S. Army and then joined the Confederate Army. Captain John C. Booth arrived in Fayetteville from Baton Rouge and assumed command of the Fayetteville Arsenal. At last, I had found a mention of Booth.

The next day I made a special trip to Fayetteville to the Museum of the Cape Fear located on the grounds of the old arsenal. There I met Bill Surface, one of the curators, who shared what information he had regarding Maj. Booth. The material was sketchy. The museum was anxious to know more about Booth. Unfortunately, Booth was commandant of the arsenal for only a brief time. He died in September of 1862 of "overwork." I promised that I would share whatever information I could find on Booth with the museum. I had no idea how I could keep that promise, as Booth seemed to be a sort of mystery man. There were many loose ends that I could not connect. The best approach to solving a difficult problem is to take a close look at the information already at hand and then go from that point. Sometimes this method leads in unexpected directions, but the results are often surprising.

John P. Booth, a lawyer, married Theresa Margaret DeWitt on May 31, 1825, in Bibb County, Georgia. Their first son, John C. Booth, was born in Macon, Georgia, June 4, 1827. In January of 1827, the senior John Booth opened up a law practice in Macon. In addition to his law office in Macon, the elder Booth also attended the Superior Courts in Lee, Muscogee, Troup, and Coweta counties in Georgia. The couple had two other children as well.

By 1831 the Booth s were living in Apalachicola, Alabama, with their three young children. On September 10, 1831, Mrs. Booth, wife of James John P. Booth, died in Woodville, Alabama, leaving her husband and their three small children. She was twenty-four years old at the time.

Little information is available on those early years, but in January of 1844, young John C. Booth and his father, and possibly other siblings, were now living in Eufaula, Barbour County, Alabama. It was from Eufaula that young Booth, then seventeen years old, wrote a letter to the Hon. J. E. Belser, Representative in the United States Congress for the Eufaula district, asking for support and recommendation in obtaining a cadet appointment to the United States Military Academy at West Point, New York. John P. Booth had previously written to the Hon. D. H. Lewis about an appointment for his son, and it is evident from young Booth's letter to Belser that while Mr. Lewis promised to obtain the appointment if possible, for some unknown reason the letter to the Hon. Lewis was misplaced. Nothing had been done to secure the desired appointment. John C. Booth's letter to Belser says:

Eufaula, Ala. Jany. 10th '44
Hon. J. E. Belser, Washington City, D. C.
"Sir
After my respects, I must beg that you will excuse me for intruding upon you, this short and uninteresting letter. – I wish to solicit your aid on a subject which to me is of considerable importance, and if it be granted, even though I should not succeed you have my sincere thanks – I am now 17 yrs. of age, and my father has not yet taken any definite course towards my future welfare. – It is now, and has been heretofore, his desire to obtain for me, an appointment in the Military Academy at West Point, but to affect this, he has never used any extraordinary exertions. – *May I ask of you the (no small) favor, that you will endeavor to obtain for* me *that appointment –*

My father wrote to the Hon. D. H. Lewis upon this subject before, and he wrote in answer that he would obtain the appointment if possible. I have his letter at the present. – If it is not convenient for you to exert your influence in my behalf, will

you mention it to that Honorable Gentleman? – I would not trouble you if I was not desirous of obtaining the appointment, as I know it would insure me a good education. –
Please answer me as soon as practicable –
I am Sir
Yours respectfully
Jno. C. Booth
(To Hon J. El Belser
Representative in Congress U. S.)"

The Hon. J. E. Belser, upon receipt of young Booth's request, wrote the following letter to President John Tyler on the back of Booth's letter:

"To the President of the United States
I rec'd a letter a few days ago, desiring me to nominate for your consideration an Individual permanently residing in my district to fill a cadet appointment. The writer of the letter on the other side of this sheet, is a youth of great promise, and I believe possessed of the necessary qualifications required in the instructions which have been sent to me. I therefore nominate John C. Booth of my district for this station if it should meet with your approval.
Yours with great respect,
J. E. Belser"

On May 9, 1844, John C. Booth received a communication from the Hon. W. Wilkins, Secretary of War, informing him that President Tyler had conferred a conditional appointment to the United States Military Academy at West Point. The acceptance of this appointment was signed by Booth and by his father, thereby binding himself to serve the United States eight years unless sooner discharged.

John C. Booth entered the Academy on July 1, 1844. Four years later, on July 1, 1848, he graduated 24th in a class of 38 cadets, and was promoted in the Army to Brevet 2nd Lieutenant in the 4th Artillery.

During the period from 1848 to 1849, Booth served in the garrison in Savannah, Georgia, and on April 9, 1849, John C. Booth and Miss Harriet Ann Williamson, daughter of John Williamson of Savannah, were married in Christ Church in Savannah. The couple would eventually have four children.

That same year, Booth was sent to the Augusta Arsenal for a brief time before participating in the Seminole War in Florida. The years from 1850-1856 were spent in moving from one military posting to another, going first to Ft. Columbus, New York; Ft. Johnston, North Carolina; frontier duty at Ft. Brady, Michigan; Ft. Brown, Texas; and finally to San Antonio, Texas, November 25, 1853. While at Ft. Brady, Booth was promoted to 1st Lieutenant in the 4th Artillery. Finally, on May 1, 1856, his eight years of service fulfilled, Booth resigned from the Army.

He accepted a position as Civil Engineer in Des Moines, Iowa, a position he held three years until he became a Clerk in the Pay Department of the Illinois Central Railroad. He held this position until 1861 when the War Between the States broke out. He resigned his position and returned home to the South where he volunteered his services to the newly-formed Confederate States Army. John C. Booth received an appointment as Captain in the Ordnance Corps of the Confederate Army. His first command was the Arsenal at Baton Rouge, Louisiana.

In 1861, the Arsenal at Fayetteville, North Carolina, was held by a small number of United States troops under the command of Lieutenant Julius Adolph DeLagnel. At that time at the Fayetteville Arsenal, there were 37,000 arms, a large number of field pieces, large quantities of powder, and machines for producing munitions. The cost of this arsenal to the United States government exceeded $ 250,000.

When the local North Carolina Governor Ellis order the

arsenal seized, state troops, led by Captain Bulla, noted for his eccentricities, surrounded the arsenal and demanded its surrender on April 22, 1861. Lieutenant Julius DeLagnel, who had only one company of light artillery at his command, inquired of Bulla as to the number of men who besieged the arsenal. Bulla replied that he had 1,000 men in troops and another 2,000 in the woods. DeLagnel saw the futility of resistance and surrendered the arsenal to the militia without firing a shot. The United States flag was lowered and state troops marched in and took command of the arsenal. The Confederate Secretary War asked the governor of North Carolina to send weapons to Virginia, and later he requested 2,000 muskets be sent to Tennessee and Arkansas regiments who were then positioned in Lynchburg, Virginia, but without arms. At the onset of the war, the South did not lack for men, but providing these men with weapons and ammunition was of utmost importance. Thus, gaining control of the Fayetteville Arsenal was of inestimable value to the Confederacy.

Since the destruction of the arsenal at Harpers Ferry, Virginia was at a severe disadvantage in supplying arms and ammunition to her troops. Twelve thousand of the 37,000 arms at Fayetteville were sent to Virginia to offset the damage incurred by the loss of the arsenal there. The Fayetteville Arsenal at that time was turning out monthly roughly five hundred rifles, and many small arms, heavy gun carriages for coastal defenses, light artillery gun carriages and caissons, as well as unlimited ammunition. As rapidly as North Carolina troops were recruited, they were armed with weapons and powder from the arsenal.

The North Carolina States troops who had originally accepted the surrender of the arsenal from DeLagnel formally relinquished command of the arsenal on June 5, 1861, turning it over to the Confederate government. Captain John C. Booth, a former United States officer with intensive experience in ordnance, was transferred from Baton Rouge and assigned command of the Fayetteville Arsenal. Booth set about assembling a company of men for guard duty. The company, formed from the 2nd Battalion N. C. Local Defense Troops, was comprised of men employed in the Ordnance Department. The company became known as "Booth's Company, Ordnance Regulars, and C. S. A." In 1862, Captain Booth was promoted to Major, Commandant of the Fayetteville Arsenal.

Many of the workers at the arsenal had previously been employed at the Harpers Ferry armory. In addition to these, there were several hundred people employed at the arsenal in a variety of jobs, some paid and others volunteers, including slaves and free blacks. A significant portion of the work force was composed of women. Rockfish Creek, a tributary of the Cape Fear River, was the site of a small defensive earthwork that was named "Fort Booth" for Major Booth, Commandant of the Arsenal. The whole complex was a scene of round-the-clock activity, providing the Confederate Army with arms, accouterments, and other necessary supplies. Maj. Booth worked incessantly to increase the capacity of the arsenal. This endeavor greatly enlarged the arsenal and generated an efficient output of weapons, but on September 6, 1862, Major John C. Booth died in Fayetteville, North Carolina, at the age of 35. A young Fayetteville woman, Miss Melinda Barge Ray who wrote in her diary on Thursday, September 11th, described his funeral:

"Major John C. Booth commandant of the Arsenal is dead. He died Saturday and was buried Sunday evening.

We had no service in our church. Pa & Ma went to the funeral. Sister & I stayed at Aunt Janes. We saw the procession go by. There more pomp & show about it than I ever saw as I never saw anything of the kind before. First came the brass band & drums then the company from fort Booth & the Arsenal guards. The co. from Fort Booth which he had formed wore crape badges on their arms, next came Rev. Joseph Huske in a barouche then the hearse & pallbearers who were those who held offices under Major Booth. They had crape streamers from their hats. Then the family of the deceased, after them all the Arsenal hands white & black & then the carriages of the friends & acquaintances. There was a great crowd. But I would not like so much show if one of my friends were to die. Major Booth's body was placed in a vault till it can be removed to Savannah."

The cause of Major Booth's untimely death was attributed to overwork. His obituary notice in the *Fayetteville Observer, Monday Evening, September 8, 1862,* noted that while Major Booth had not resided in Fayetteville very long, the short time that he was there left a favorable impression the citizens there. He was greatly respected for both his extensive business at the arsenal, as well as for his social qualities. The obituary stated, "He was a graduate of West Point, a gentleman of decided ability, and of as large and comprehensive views as any one whom it has been our fortune to know, and if his health been good and his life spared, it would have been his pride and pleasure to make the Arsenal the great reservoir from which the Confederacy would draw its means of offence and defense…He leaves a wife and four children."

Col. J. A. DeLagnel, who had originally surrendered the arsenal to the state militia, and who had then joined the Confederacy, succeeded Booth a commandant.

In 1865, Sherman's armies marched into Fayetteville, its primary mission the destruction of the Arsenal. It would take 1,000 Union soldiers, under Gen. Orlando M. Poe, to take the Arsenal that was held primarily by women at that time. One of Sherman's staff officers described the arsenal as being in "good repair," and while similar in design to the one in Washingt5on, was "smaller, but with more taste." Sherman commanded that it be totally destroyed, saying that he did not want a single brick left of the U. S. Arsenal that had been converted to serve the Rebels. The troops burned and smashed the twenty structures that made up the Fayetteville Arsenal, thus ending it valuable service to the Confederacy. Today only scattered brick and stone mark the site of the Fayetteville Arsenal. The site itself is part of the Museum of the Cape Fear complex.

In 1878, Booth's wife, in response to a request for information from General George W. Cullum who was compiling a West Point Directory, listed consumption as the cause of her husband's death. Mrs. Booth also stated in her letter of February 6, 1878, that Major John C. Booth was later buried in her family graveyard near Savannah, Georgia.

This graveyard is located on what was once part of Brampton Plantation, an old Savannah River rice and cotton plantation dating from the late 1700s. An early planter from South Carolina, Jonathan Bryan, had established it. John Williamson, Mrs. Booth's father, purchased the land in 1848. In December of 1864, Sherman's soldiers destroyed the plantation, burning the residences. The home was never replaced. In 1910, the property became an industrial site. The family graveyard, surrounded by a high brick wall, has been preserved, though vandals have wreaked a good bit of damage over the years. There are currently about fourteen tombstones, the earliest of which is dated 1783. The latest stone is dated 1862, that of Major Booth. The burial of Harriet Williamson Booth may also be on this site, but if so, no tombstone marks her grave.

A bit of speculation suggests that when Union soldiers burned the residence, those living there at the time, which may have included Mrs. Booth and her children, were forced to find another place to live. They possibly left Savannah entirely. The 1878 letter Mrs. Booth wrote to General Cullum was written from "Carlyle," but there is nothing else to indicate exactly where "Carlyle" was located. There are several Carlyles from which to choose. The catch, however, is finding the right

Carlyle.

In the way of a postscript to this story, on May 2, 2004, Savannah Chapter 2 of the United Daughters of the Confederacy held a formal grave dedication in the small cemetery where Booth lies. A representative from the West Point Society of Savannah, Col. Eric Robyn, gave a brief address at the grave of the former West Point graduate, and a Confederate battle flag was placed on the grave. A contingent of soldiers from the 22nd Georgia Infantry fired a volley, and taps were played over the site where this son of Dixie quietly sleeps, awaiting the final roll call.

The dedication of Booth's grave

A Real Confederate Daughter

Those people who are most familiar with the oldest women's organization in the United States, the Southern heritage organization known as the United Daughters of the Confederacy®, know the esteem and respect with which we view a lady who is given the designation, Real Daughter. The qualification to attain this designation is quite simple – the lady in question *must* be the daughter of a Confederate soldier. Obviously, in the 21st Century, there are few who can make this claim, and with each year that passes, that number dwindles. At this writing, there are only eight Real Daughters still living in the state of Georgia. There are still a few living in other states as well. It is of one of these that I include here, because she is a member of the Savannah Chapter 2, UDC. Here is her story:

Richard Johnson was born in 1850 in Warren County, Georgia. When he was little more than ten years old, young Richard enlisted as a Private in Company K of the Warren County Georgia Militia at the Augusta Powder Works. There, along with other young boys, he worked as a "powder monkey" making gunpowder for the Confederacy. He also served in the 46th Georgia Infantry, Price's Brigade of Muscogee County, Georgia. He served in the Confederate Army until 1864 when he was discharged.

Johnson later married Rainie Alligood, born in 1890 in Toombs County, Georgia, and on August 13, 1919, a daughter they named Katie was born to them. Rainie taught Katie how to quilt, a skill that would serve her well in later years. At the age of 16, Katie Johnson married Jethro Love on December 8, 1935. Together the couple had ten children, two of whom died in infancy.

Richard Johnson died in 1944 at the ripe old age of 94. He was buried in Montgomery County, Georgia, in the Sharpe Cemetery. This small cemetery is located about six miles from Alston, Georgia.

Katie Love, who was approaching her 89th year in 2008, lives with a daughter and her husband in Santa Claus, Georgia.

Katie Love

This small community is situated on the outskirts of Lyons, Georgia. Katie occupied her time by making hand-sewn quilts, most of which portray the Confederate Battle Flag. She sold these from her home and they are in great demand throughout the state. They have special appeal to collectors because they are handmade by a real Confederate daughter.

On August 31, 2011, Katie Love passed away peacefully, surrounded by her large family. She was laid to rest in the Sharpe Cemetery in Montgomery County, Georgia. On May 19, 2013, a group of ladies from Savannah Chapter 2, of the United Daughters of the Confederacy, held a grave marking ceremony at her grave and also placed an Southern Cross of Honor on the grave of her father, Richard Johnson. Thus, another Daughter of Dixie was finally honored.

George W. Washington

The story of George Washington is told here in the words of his great-granddaughter, Georgia Wright Benton of Savannah, Georgia.

"My great-grandfather, George W. Washington, a slave, was born March 31, 1845, on the McQueen Plantation in Sumter County, South Carolina. He would have been about 16 years old when he went off to war as the body servant of his young master, Lieutenant William Alexander McQueen, who was then 22 years old. Lt. Alex McQueen was born in Sumter, South Carolina, and was the son of a Presbyterian minister. He commanded a cannon and crew of Garden's Battery from Sumter. These two men, slave and master would serve together for four long years. During these years they participated in several major battles of the war, three of which were the Battle of Sharpsburg, the Battle of the Crater at Petersburg, Virginia, and the Battle of Gettysburg. It was at Gettysburg that Lt. McQueen was wounded, and my great-grandfather brought him safely home to Sumter to recuperate from his wounds. Please remember that my great-grandfather had numerous opportunities to escape to the North, but it was his personal choice to serve with his beloved childhood friend."

On April 5, 1865, Union Brigadier General Edward E. Potter, with about 2700 fighting men marched from Georgetown along the river road burning mills, gins and cotton, and stripping farms and plantations of their livestock

189

and food. Thus, at the very end of the war, all of the atrocities of the war came to Sumter District.

Meanwhile, news of Potter's raiding party had reached Sumter and orders were issued for the local militia to assemble. Old men, teenage boys, and convalescent soldiers from the hospitals answered the call to arms, a total of about 575 men. Among them was Lt. McQueen and his loyal companion and body servant, George Washington.

On a Saturday morning, April 9, 1865, the same day of Lee's surrender at Appomattox, news of which had not yet reached Sumter that the war was over, General Potter's troops arrived at Dingle's Mill where they were at first driven back by Sumter's defenders. Soon however, it became obvious that resistance was impossible and Sumter's militia was forced to retreat. It was during this last stand that Lt. McQueen was struck and killed by cannon fire.

"George W. Washington performed his final duties to his fallen master. He brought Alex McQueen's body home to the McQueen family for burial."

"George Washington very likely stayed on with the McQueen family for a time. In 1872 he married Violet Davis. In 1873 he began working as a servant and butler with the A. A. Solomons, a prominent Jewish family in Sumter. He served the Solomons for 38 years. In 1885, his daughter Mamie Washington, my grandmother was born."

"George W. Washington died January 27, 1911. He was buried in the Walker Cemetery in Sumter, not very far from Alex McQueen's grave. The Solomons family had a marker erected on his grave which recounts his service with Lt. McQueen in the War Between the States, and also his service with the Solomons family."

"In October 2005, the General P. T. G. Beauregard Camp No. 1458, of the Sons of Confederate Veterans repaired the grave marker and held a dedication ceremony honoring Washington for his faithful service and upright life."

As a sort of footnote to this story, I feel that it is important that I add the final chapter to this story. On December 13, 2013, Georgia Edna Wright Benton was presented her certificate of membership in the Savannah Chapter 2, United Daughters of the Confederacy, of which she is a valued member. She is not the first African-American woman to hold membership in this prestigious organization. There are others who are members in other states. However, she does enjoy the distinction of being the first in Georgia. At present, Georgia's son, Leroy Benton is in the process of applying for membership in the Sons of Confederate Veterans.

Georgia W. Benton receiving her UDC certificate, Savannah, 12/14/2013

Is That Really General Lee?

If ever a living man resembled the iconic and noble General Robert Edward Lee, it would have to be James M. Adams who with great regularity is called upon to play this role. The resemblance of Mr. Adams to Lee is nothing short of uncanny. Donning a gray general's uniform or perhaps period civilian, he easily slips into the persona of Lee – he becomes Lee. In both physical appearance and demeanor, his performance is flawless. The clock eerily runs backwards to Lee as the young lieutenant who supervised the building of Fort Pulaski, or to the Lee who visited his old friend General Johnston in Savannah after the war. But who is this man who oversteps[1] the bounds of time to resurrect that most beloved Southerner of all, Robert Edward Lee?

Jim Adams was born in the small Appalachian town of Norton, Virginia, August 16, 1933. He spent six years combined active military service in the United States Army and in the United States Navy. His higher education was obtained at East Tennessee State College and graduate work at Ohio State University. It was during his time in Ohio that Jim became interested in the history of the War Between the States. He became a Confederate Cavalry re-enactor. It was not long before people with whom he came in contact during the re-enactments noticed Jim's uncanny resemblance to Robert E. Lee. When he appeared in a PBS series on the Civil War, Jim's friends, co-workers, and students began calling him the "General."

After retiring from education, Jim and his wife Jeanne,

also a retired teacher, moved to Savannah. It was in Savannah that Jim joined the 22nd Georgia Heavy Artillery unit and began reenacting as a member of a cannon crew. He also worked part time at Old Fort Jackson, where his resemblance to Lee was quickly noticed. It was at this point that Jim decided to "become" General Lee.

In the persona of Lee, Jim Adams has given many first person presentations at General Lee for Elderhostel groups, Civil War Round Tables, and various history related organizations and groups, including the Battle of Olustee Festival in Lake City, Florida. He has portrayed that revered Lee in numerous festivals in Georgia, South Carolina, Florida, and Virginia.

Jim Adams as General Robert E. Lee

A prolific writer and historian, Adams has published three books on local history and is presently engaged in writing a fourth book. For a number of years, Jim wrote more than 350 columns for the *Savannah Morning News*, which he called "Historically Speaking" One of his books, *Entwined Destinies – West Point and the Coastal Empire 1802-2002* caught the attention of the United States Military Academy at West Point, New York. He was invited to come to West Point where he was honored by being named a Friend of West Point, a singular honor that is very rarely bestowed. While at West Point, Jim, as Robert E. Lee, lectured to a class of cadets on Lee's days as a cadet at the Academy, and then later as Superintendent of the Academy..

His role as Lee has brought other recognition to Jim. In 2004, the Savannah Chapter of the United Daughters of the Confederacy® bestowed the coveted Jefferson Davis Gold Medal, which is the highest award that can be present by that organization to a non-member. In December of 2006, that same organization elected him an Honorary Associate Member of the Savannah Chapter No. 2, UDC. He is also an honorary member of the West Point Society of Savannah. On Robert E. Lee's 200th birthday, January 19, 2007, the Sons of Confederate Veterans and the Military Order of the Stars and Bars, chose to have Jim Adams to be the keynote speaker. For that occasion, he portrayed Lee after the war.

Being a native Virginian, it is perhaps no accident, that James Mack Adams so closely resembles that other native Virginian who led the Army of Northern Virginia during the War Between the States. Certainly, for a man who once told me that he had two strong ambitions in his youth – one, to attend the U. S. Military Academy at West Point; and two, failing to accomplish that, he longed to attend Virginia Military Institute. Although these two desires were not accomplished in the usual manner, Jim has attained at least the first of those ambitions on a path "less traveled." Highly respected and honored for his portrayal of General Lee, his alter ego has opened doors undreamed of. Perhaps, the real General Lee is keeping an eye on his protégé down in Savannah.

Who's/Whose Bones?

Laurel Grove Cemetery North is a magnificent old Victorian cemetery, which opened in 1852 as a municipal cemetery. Situated on the site of the old Spring Hill Plantation, it was established to fill an urgent need when Colonial Park Cemetery was closed to burials due to lack of space. Through the years, Laurel Grove has attracted thousands of tourists who come to see and photograph its beautiful old monuments and to visit the graves of the various notables who rest beneath the moss-draped trees. Its wide carriage paths wind past the graves of Anna Davenport Raines, co-founder of UDC; Juliette Gordon Low, founder of the Girl Scouts; Florence Martus, the well-known "Waving Girl"; James Pierpont, composer of "Jingle Bells"; Gen. Francis S. Bartow, CSA; the famed "Gettysburg Lot"; and others too numerous to name. The ironwork and marble statuary add their opulence to this gem of cemetery artwork.

However, not all of the graves are indicated by fanciful monuments. Indeed, many of them bear no markers at all. One such section on the north side has been designated at burial space for indigents. Some of these graves do bear modest markers, but many more are unmarked. One of the burials in this section does have a flat marble marker, but its presence has created a mystery that is still unsolved at this writing. No one seems to know where it came from, and exactly what it marks.

The inscription on the stone reads:

SPD BONES
29 March 90

195

At first glance, it would appear that one of the canine members of the Savannah Police Department K-9 Unit rests here. Traditionally, municipal cemeteries discourage the interment of animals in a lot designed for humans. The prevailing theory suggests that this was a fairly important dog, or at least one who died under impressive circumstances, and thus an exception was made. Talking with cemetery personnel revealed that none of them knew anything about this mysterious burial. No record exists in the cemetery office, which keeps records of every burial in the cemetery.

In an attempt to learn more about "Bones," I contacted a person who had helped me locate information for my earlier books, Corporal William S. Ray, of the Savannah-Chatham Metropolitan Police Department. Corporal Ray put me in touch with Sergeant Gregory Ernst who is with the present K-9 Unit. After talking with several officers who served in the K-9 Unit in 1990, Sgt. Ernst told me that not a single officer knew anything about the grave. He also told me that the police department kept very good records on their canines and they had never had a canine named "Bones."

So now, all this begs the questions, "Whose Bones?" Are these human bones or are they the bones of a canine? Does this stone actually mark the spot where some errant bones from the Savannah Police Department are buried? Were the bones discovered somewhere, never identified, and just buried here? Is this, in fact, the grave of a K-9 whose handler felt deserved a respectable burial in a prestigious cemetery? If this latter question merits an affirmative answer, then why not bury the dog, if it is a dog, in the police lot at Laurel Grove, a lot that bears the ominous number 911?

This mysterious grave leaves many questions unanswered. Of course, since the stone in question is located in an area set aside for indigents, perhaps it marks the grave of some poor unfortunate who was known to the police by the street name, "Bones."

In any case, the fact remains that burials in the cemetery, and the subsequent placement of a marker on the grave should leave a paper trail. Burials are always recorded in the cemetery department's records. Was this the clandestine burial of an unknown corpse by unknown parties? Whatever the final answer is, the grave adds another legend to the hauntingly beautiful Laurel Grove Cemetery.

Harlem Blues

Situated about halfway between Augusta and Thomson, Georgia, Harlem is a little bedroom community of about 2,000 residents. It grew up along the Georgia Railroad toward the latter part of the 19th century, incorporating as a town October 24, 1870. It got its name at the suggestion of a New York visitor who came down to stay with some relatives in the area. The New Yorker thought the town resembled the then elite artistic section of New York City known as Harlem.

There being only one major industry in Harlem, the Tracey-Luckey Pecan Factory that buys pecans and packages pecan products for sale around the world, most of Harlem's residents make their living at various jobs in Augusta and at Fort Gordon. The small sleepy Southern town's proximity to Fort Gordon and Augusta makes it attractive to military retirees as well. Highway 220 or Louisville Road, which runs through the center of the small business district, is the main thoroughfare. Most of the businesses – a florist, gift shop, realtor's office, restaurant, drugstore, barbershop and beauty salon, police station, bank, several antique shops, pecan factory, museum, dentist's office, and post office – are located along Louisville Road. The town also boasts a high school on the outskirts of the city limit, an elementary school, and a middle school. A small public library is located in an old Victorian era cottage. The three main churches are Baptist, Methodist, and Episcopal. There is a Church of the Latter Day Saints as well.

Highway 78, known locally as the Gordon Highway

because Fort Gordon fronts on it as one nears Augusta, crosses Highway 220 and runs in a north-south direction. Along this highway, within the city limits may be found a couple of service stations, a couple of restaurants, and a small antique mall. A railroad track bisects the business area, and trains pass through on regularly scheduled runs.

Harlem, like many small communities has had its share of characters over its one hundred plus years of existence. While these individuals had no direct claim to any outstanding deeds or contributions to society as a whole, their lives give flavor and texture to the town they chose to call home. When my husband and I lived there in the 1970s and 80s, we were privileged to know some of these people whose eccentricities left a lasting impression on our memories of that small town.

One such person was our neighbor who owned and operated a small motel just across the street from our house. Helen Davie was an imposing elderly widow who lived in part of the building that housed the motel. She seldom ventured out of her motel, preferring to live quietly with her two dogs, the very elderly little Miami and a much, much larger nondescript hulk of a dog she called Red Eye. The motel itself had about six or eight units, and being located right on Highway 220, the motel was a convenient stop for truckers and others passing through town.

We had not lived in our house very long before we began witnessing events that whetted our curiosity. In late afternoon and early evening, the VACANCY sign appeared at the entrance to the motel. As soon as one or two rooms were rented for the night, the NO VACANCY sign appeared, even though there were obviously several other vacant rooms. Eventually we learned that our neighbor was quite fond of passing away her evenings in her own living quarters with her cigarettes and a bottle of her favorite spirits. When enough revenue had been taken in to cover the cost of a bottle, she put up the NO VACANCY sign, thus insuring that she would not be disturbed the rest of the night. Despite any mental picture a reader may envision of a well-bred proper old lady, Mrs. Davie was possessed of an extensive and quite colorful vocabulary that could shame a trucker, and sometimes did when they inadvertently stopped there for a night.

Red Eye, apparently not too fond of his mistress's habits of imbibing in the evenings, would leave home and roam the streets of Harlem. Being of considerable bulk and size, he had no difficulty strolling across Highway 220 despite the heavy traffic. We would frequently hear the squeal of air brakes as a passing trucker slowed down to accommodate Red Eye's slow ambling stroll across the street. No trucker was willing to risk hitting Red Eye and bringing down the wrath of Red Eye's mistress on his head.

At some point, Mrs. Davie would realize that Red Eye had left home and was out on the streets. She solved such a problem quite easily. She would pick up the phone, call the police and ask them to pick up Red Eye. A small town police department at that time knew most of the local people. When they received a call from one of the townspeople, they rarely had to ask for the address, nor did they go through much of the red tape that seems to burden many municipal offices.

Within a short time after Mrs. Davie phoned in her request, we would be treated to the sight of a police cruiser pulling into the parking lot of the motel. The officer would get out of the cruiser and open the back door of the car. Out would lumber old Red Eye who would then go to the door of the motel and wait for the officer to let him in. One police officer was overhead to say, wistfully, and hopefully in jest, "One of these days I'm going to shoot that damn dog." This was a regular occurrence, and regardless of their personal opinions of the dog duty being foisted on them, the police never failed to bring Red Eye home unharmed. It is not too much of a stretch of the imagination to guess that perhaps Red Eye liked to think of himself as an unofficial member of the police department and enjoyed his ride.

Harlem did not have a Catholic church. The nearest one was in Thomson, about ten miles away. It became our habit to go to Sunday Mass, and then have Sunday dinner at the Belle Meade Country Club. Mrs. Davie held a social membership at the club, and she too would have here Sunday dinner there. When she had finished with her meal, she would ask for a doggie bag, and place any meat scraps in the bag. It was after she had salvaged scraps from her plate that she would then get up and stroll around the dining room, eyeing everyone's plate. If she spotted a likely morsel, she would snatch it off the unsuspecting patron's plate and pop it into the doggie bag. In a few memorable instances, the targeted person was still eating his meal when the meat-snatching occurred. Red Eye did indeed live "high on the hog."

There came a time when Mrs. Davie, along with a few of her cronies, decided to take a trip to Miami, Florida. Mrs. Davie, ever mindful of her responsibilities as the owner of two canine companions, first made provisions for the care of her pets while she was out of town. Red Eye was rather easy to make arrangements for, but little Miami was another story. Miami was quite old and feeble, and his days were obviously numbered. Mrs. Davie made a call to the local funeral home and requested that the funeral home owner meet her at the Harlem Cemetery.

When he arrived at the Davie lot in the cemetery, Mrs. Davie was already there. She explained that she was going out of town and that she was concerned that little Miami might not survive while she was gone.

"If Miami should die before I return, I want you to get a casket, place Miami in it, and I want him buried on this lot, at the foot of my husband's grave. I also want a stone placed there to mark the grave." Barrett Prather was appalled, and when he was finally able to speak, replied to this unusual request.

"Helen," he protested, "what you are asking me to do would be very expensive. It would cost a great deal of money, and I am not sure if it is even legal to bury a dog in this cemetery."

In a voice that brooked no argument whatsoever, she emphatically responded, "I want this done, damn it. It's my damn lot and my damn money!" As far as she was concerned, the matter was settled. As things eventually turned out, the matter was settled.

The ladies decided that the best way to go on their trip to Miami was to drive themselves. Considering the age of these ladies and their widely known driving skills, (or lack thereof) this idea fell short of the miraculous. They set out on their adventure on a Saturday morning. That same morning, my husband had walked down to Prather's Restaurant on Main Street where he joined a group of men that met there every Saturday morning for coffee, gossip, and conversation on the latest happenings both locally and beyond. While he was sitting there, the county sheriff walked in and sat down at the table with the other men. In the course of the conversation, the sheriff made the comment that he had stopped a car headed toward the McDuffie County line. The car caught his attention when he noticed it was moving rather erratically down the highway, sometimes speeding, then slowing down, and sometimes weaving slightly. When he pulled the car over, he discovered that there were three elderly ladies in car, one of whom was talking and driving. After checking the license and questioning them, he allowed them to go on their way. He offered his opinion that he hoped they were not traveling very far.

"Sheriff Tankersley, those ladies are on their way to Miami," my husband told him.

"Miami, Florida?" he replied. "Hell, the way they are driving, they won't make it to Thomson."

Well, the ladies did get to Florida and back. Little Miami did live to see his mistress return home. Red Eye continued his usual nocturnal perambulations around Harlem, occasionally interrupted in his strolls when a passing police car would pick him up and return him to his mistress.

We were not in Harlem when little Miami finally died, but sometime ago, I visited the cemetery in Harlem to help a group that was taking an inventory for the purpose of listing all of the burials there. At the Davie lot, between the foot of Mrs. Davie's husband's grave and that of her own, I noticed a small stone engraved with the name "Miami." Of Red Eye, there was nothing to indicate where he now rests. Knowing Mrs. Davie, I am quite certain that little Miami's remains are interred there near his mistress. After all, it was her "damn money."

Another of Harlem's characters in residence was an old man named C. M. Blanchard. When I first knew him, he and his wife lived in an old rambling house just west of the business district. Their two children, a son and daughter, had long since established homes and families of their own, and the couple lived quietly there. Both were quite well known for their penurious ways. Their daughter-in-law once told how the Blanchards, who owned a number of rental houses in the area, dealt with a fire that destroyed one of these rental houses. One Thanksgiving Day, the family had just sat down to a traditional Thanksgiving dinner, when they received word that one of the tenant houses had caught fire. The volunteer fire department was notified and the whole family rushed to the scene and discovered that the tenants were not at home. In an attempt to try to save some of the tenant's possessions, Blanchard's son and daughter-in-law began to pull out what possessions they could safely reach. It soon became apparent that the fire would destroy the house, even though the firefighters were working desperately to save it.

Mr. Blanchard watched with tears in his eyes, bemoaning the fact that he did not have insurance on it. His wife heard his remark, and, in a high-pitched voice, rather timidly contradicted him, saying, "Yes, it does. I took out a policy on it last month."

With evident joy replacing his tears, Mr. Blanchard shouted to the struggling firefighters, "Let it burn, boys. Let it burn!"

This was the same irascible and frugal old man, who once suffered from an upset stomach. He went to the local drugstore and bought a bottle of Pepto Bismol. When he got home, he opened the bottle and took a generous dose. A short time later, his stomach having returned to its normal state, he took the bottle back to the drugstore and demanded a refund on the unused portion.

As town characters go, Harlem was not deficient in its share. Probably two of the most colorfully vocal were Ruth Connor and her daughter, Polly Connor Clary. These two, along with Polly's husband Dick, had gone to the dogs a long time ago. Quite literally. When I knew these three, they were owners of twenty-seven Chihuahuas, seven of which were champion show dogs. At least one of these champions was shown at the famed Westminster Dog Show in Madison Square Garden in New York City. The Clarys never sold a single puppy, but kept all of them in a special room, lined with dog crates and dog show trophies. A large fenced yard provided plenty of room for the dogs to run. No children were ever cared for as well as those Chihuahuas.

Mary Virginia Connor, or Polly, as she preferred to be called, was a feisty redhead, who was born in 1928 in Columbia County, Georgia. She was the daughter of Otis and Ruth Crowell Connor. Her father was a farmer and a blacksmith who also clandestinely operated a whiskey still on the banks of the Savannah River, up in the Appling-Winfield area.

After the family moved to Harlem, they opened a small restaurant near the present day post office. In addition to the restaurant business, Otis Connor also ran an ambulance service and an undertaking business. Polly grew up here and attended Georgia Southern College in Statesboro for a short time. At some very early age, Polly acquired a vocabulary that became her trademark. Perhaps she inherited it from her Irish father. She frequently sprinkled her speech with expletives, coupled with highly colorful phrases. Indeed, her father would proudly remark on appropriate occasions that he did not need to worry about Polly as she was quite capable of taking care of herself should the need arise.

Never at loss for words, she could render any sailor or modern biker speechless with her original phrases and cuss words. Brave, indeed, were the souls who dared to cross her. Even her employer, owner of the Chevrolet place in Thomson, cringed when she got her Irish up. One of her well-known scathing remarks of someone who made the mistake of questioning her judgment was, "He couldn't pour piss out of a goddamn boot unless it had the instructions written on the bottom!" When Polly really got wound up, ladies gasped in horror, while brawny men turned pale. She was certainly never a shrinking violet. Her vocabulary and unique turn of phrase were legendary.

Dick Clary grew up in Harlem, went to the University of Georgia, and received a degree from that institution. He had been a coach in public schools in the area. When he retired from education, he spent much of his time going to dog shows with his wife and mother-in-law, and puttering around the house. This lifestyle soon began to wear on him, and he entered the mayoral race in Harlem and won the election by a landslide. His method of politicking was to have some small cards printed up asking people to vote for him. The cards were then distributed to various shops and businesses. This method worked and Dick saw no reason to change his tactics in later elections. He did not call upon people and ask for their vote, nor did he actively advertise in the media. He probably was the only politician who did not aggressively campaign for an office. The office of Mayor carried the additional duties of magistrate in many small Georgia towns. In this capacity, Dick held traffic court in Harlem on a regular basis. His brother Ed owned the local bank.

Mrs. Connor, Miss Ruth to most Harlem folks, had her own idiosyncrasies. She was a tiny little lady with snow-white hair when I first met her. Her vocabulary was as unique and as extensive as that of her daughter. Her babies were her dogs. She once told me of how as a young girl she loved horses. Born in 1897 and married young at the age of sixteen, she often rode bareback in the area known as Heggie Rock.

This particular area of Columbia County was formed from a vast granite outcropping, believed to be a "root" of Stone Mountain. It was a popular place for picnics in the late 1800s and early 1900s. Access to Heggie Rock was eventually closed to the general public in order to protect and preserve the rare flora found there. Ruth Connor would often leave her baby Polly in the care of a nurse and ride her horse over the countryside. When the baby's normal feeding time would arrive, Ruth would return to the house and the nurse would hand the baby up to her. Ruth, still mounted on the horse, would then nurse Polly.

After the death of Otis Connor in 1956, Ruth lived with Polly and Dick. I knew her in her much later years. When my husband and I visited the Clarys, "Miss Ruth" was always there. Before she retired for the evening, Miss Ruth made several trips to the "dog room" and picked up five or six small carriers and their occupants, which she then took to her room. These favored ones would sleep that night in the lap of luxury. She was also the official undertaker when one of the wee dogs passed away. Such an event threw the whole family into mourning. Miss Ruth once confided to me that when she died, she did not particularly care if anyone showed up for her funeral. However, she did want all of her dogs placed in cars and taken to the cemetery for her burial. She wanted her burial to take place at sunset, with her dogs as chief mourners. Miss Ruth died peacefully in her sleep at home in 1986, and although John and I attended the funeral, I cannot recall if any Chihuahuas were present.

Some years ago, a group of local citizens was discussing possibilities for revitalizing Harlem. A brainstorming session initiated as various locals contributed their ideas to enhance the little town. The local Episcopal priest at that time offered a suggestion that since the Tracey-Luckey Pecan Factory was the only industry on the block, perhaps a Nut Festival would be appropriate. While this suggestion drew quite a few chuckles, one wag observed that Harlem had enough nuts already and he didn't see the point in celebrating that facet of Harlem as it would likely just encourage more of the same.

From this discussion, however, came the seeds for an annual festival, the Oliver Hardy Festival. This festival honors Oliver Norvell Hardy, known to old movie buffs as the partner of Stan Laurel in the old Laurel and Hardy movies.

Oliver Norvell Hardy was born in Harlem, Georgia, January 18, 1892. His parents are buried in the Harlem Cemetery. Originally named Norvell, he was the son of Oliver

Hardy and Emily Norvell who had married in 1890. Hardy's father died a little over a year after Norvell was born, and his mother moved to Madison and then to Milledgeville where she was employed as a hotel manager. Although, by all accounts, Hardy was not much of a scholar, running away and dropping out of several schools, he did have a musical talent that he pursued until he discovered the world of motion pictures.

The Laurel & Hardy Mural in Harlem, Georgia

Grants and private donations eventually led to the establishment of an Oliver Hardy Museum. The festival attracts people from all over and is a yearly event, and includes opportunities to see old Laurel and Hardy movies at the museum, arts and crafts exhibits, and all of the usual activities associated with festivals of this nature.

Before I leave this quaint little community, it is perhaps fitting that I mention one tidbit gleaned from the 1996 September/October issue of a publication, *Georgia Journal,* which adds another brief page to Harlem's history. The article in question centered on an African-American musician, Thomas Million Turpin. Tom Turpin was born in Savannah, Georgia, June 18, 1873. He was the son of "Honest John" and Lula Turpin. About 1880, the Turpin family moved to St. Louis, and it was there that John Turpin opened a saloon. It was also there in St. Louis that young Tom taught himself to play the piano. Tom and his older brother Charles invested in a gold mine in Nevada, but this venture proved to be unsuccessful and the two returned to St. Louis where young Tom opened up the Rosebud Café and Bar, an establishment that soon became a popular meeting place for musicians like Scott Joplin and others in that period of American musical history often referred to as the "Gay Nineties."

In 1897, Tom Turpin became the first African-American composer to publish a ragtime tune he called "Harlem Rag Two-Step." This piece brought instant recognition to the young composer, and the birth of ragtime at the Rosebud Bar made it the "in place" to be. Turpin's style of standing at the keyboard, pounding out the syncopated rhythms became legendary. Turpin held piano contests that lasted hours, and in some cases, even days, where pianists from all over the country competed against each other to invent new styles and melodies in the popular ragtime genre.

Some historians now believe that "Harlem Rag" was so-named in honor of the little Georgia town of Harlem. Harlem, New York, at that period was a rather upscale white community, and it is believed that it would be unlikely for Turpin to have written music about that area. It would only be much later that Harlem, New York, would become a minority community.

Tom Turpin died in St. Louis, Missouri, August 13, 1922. He only published four other ragtime compositions: "The Bowery Buck" in 1899; "A Ragtime Nightmare" in 1900; "The St. Louis Rag" in 1903; and "The Buffalo Rag" in 1904.

Just a Little Girl

She was only thirteen years old that fateful morning Mary Phagan boarded the streetcar that would take her from Bellwood into Atlanta. It was a special day for her, for it was Confederate Memorial Day in Georgia, April 26, 1913, and in Atlanta as all over Georgia, there would be parades and memorial services. In 1913, many Confederate veterans were still living, and this day had special significance for them. More than 200 Confederate veterans would don their old gray uniforms and march in a procession down Peachtree Street. On that day, the widow of General Stonewall Jackson would be present to accept the salute. It was a legal holiday across Georgia, and businesses were closed to honor the Confederate dead.

Little Mary Phagan had been born in 1900 in Marietta, Georgia, to Fanny and John Phagan. John Phagan was a tenant farmer, and when the cotton market fell drastically, the farm could no longer stay in operation and was sold. He found himself without a means of earning a living. He moved his family away from Marietta to the small textile mill community of Bellwood, just outside Atlanta, where John worked in one of the textile mills. His children were also employed in the mill for five cents an hour. Such mill workers were often referred to as "lint heads" from the cotton lint that clung to the clothing and hair of those who worked in the mills. John Phagan died in 1911, and Fanny married J.W. Coleman within a year of John Phagan's death.

Though young, Mary had been able to find a job in the

National Pencil Company in Atlanta where she earned the princely sum of twelve cents an hour. On the morning in question, Mary's plans were to stop by the pencil factory where she worked and collect her pay. She then intended to watch the Confederate Memorial Day parade on Peachtree Street.

And so on that fateful April 26, Mary intended to collect her pay from the pencil factory and then watch the parade in Atlanta. With this plan in mind, she set out on the streetcar for Atlanta. She arrived there about noon, and went to the factory, where she discovered that the manager who usually paid her was not there. Leo Frank, the superintendent of the pencil factory, however was there and he paid Mary, who hurried away, intent on seeing the parade. Mr. Frank left a short time later and went home for lunch. Leo Frank returned from his lunch, and locked the factory when he left at six o'clock that day, after speaking to the Negro night watchman, Newt Lee.

It was about 3:30 a.m. when Newt Lee descended to the basement of the factory to use the toilet. As he flashed his lantern about the basement, which was cluttered with packing crates, boxes of imperfect pencils, and coal, he suddenly spotted something in a corner that appeared to be a bundle of rags. As he approached closer, however, the lantern light revealed the body of a young girl, a little over four feet in height, with blood-matted hair and a cord tied tightly around her neck. She had also suffered severe trauma to the back of her head. Lee hurriedly ran back upstairs and attempted to call Mr. Frank on the telephone, but there was no answer. Newt Lee then asked the telephone operator to get the police. Within fifteen minutes, the police and a reporter had reached the factory crime scene.

As was perhaps typical in that period of our history, the police arrested Newt Lee on the spot after finding some pencil-written notes that seemed to implicate Lee. It was not long afterwards, however, that Leo Frank came under suspicion due to his nervousness and seemingly unusual behavior. He was also a Yankee Jew, and that fact tended to exacerbate matters. Before the uproar caused by Mary's death had barely begun, yet a third person was implicated in her death, a Negro named Jim Conley who also worked at the factory. All three men – Newt Lee, Jim Conley, and Leo Frank – were arrested, but in the end, it was Leo Frank who was ultimately found guilty by the jury, despite a lack of concrete evidence.

Anti-Semitism played a major role in the Leo Frank case. The South was struggling to pull itself out of a depressed economy. The fact that Frank was the product of a wealthy Northern Jewish family was a mark against him in the eyes of many poor Southerners. Few were aware that Leo Frank's uncle, to whom he wrote on that Confederate Memorial Day and which was introduced in court as evidence against him, knew that the uncle, Moses Frank was a Confederate veteran. Mention of this fact was carefully avoided in the prosecutor's speech to the jury. Frank's remark in the letter mentioned the holiday and the "thin gray line" of the Confederate veterans in a way that seemed to make fun of the veterans in the eyes of the jury.

Although the evidence pointed to Jim Conley as the perpetrator of the crime, Conley leveled an accusation of sexual perversion against Leo Frank. The charge of sexual perversion was tantamount to a death sentence in the South in 1913. Testimony by a brothel owner, which was likely a police-coerced statement, helped to implicate Frank by stating that he told Mrs. Formby that he needed a room in her establishment for the purpose of reviving a young girl who fell and hit her head. Mrs. Formby further declared that Leo Frank had visited her establishment in the past. The idea of Leo Frank or anyone else for that matter, walking through the streets of Atlanta carrying the body of a young girl seems utterly absurd today. Before the trial of Frank began, Mrs. Formby had repudiated former statements she made in the affidavit to the police, but the damage was done. Jim Conley testified against

Frank, and history was made in the South. For the first time in history, a white man was convicted of murder on the testimony of a black man. Leo Frank was sentenced to hang.

The fact that the evidence was skewed or nonexistent and the investigation was botched and constructed by the police involved in the investigation does not mitigate the outcome. Leo Frank was found guilty of the murder of Mary Phagan, despite reservations by Judge Leonard Roan who was not comfortable with the guilty verdict.

Judge Roan believed Frank was innocent of the crime and had confided this belief to close friends. Roan wanted to grant a motion for a new trial, but legal experts reminded him that the outcome would be unchanged. Frank's only hope lay in the pardoning authority of the Governor of the State of Georgia. On June 21, 1915, Governor John M. Slaton commuted the death penalty to life imprisonment for Frank.

The Georgians who had flocked to Atlanta for the trial were incensed when they learned that Governor Slaton had commuted Frank's sentence. Five thousand citizens marched on the governor's mansion in Buckhead to proclaim their dissatisfaction with Governor Slaton. The police had difficulty controlling the crowds, in part because most of the police were in sympathy with the mob that came to the mansion. Tom Watson, a newspaperman who wielded considerable clout in Georgia at that time, accused Governor Slaton of being a traitor. Watson not only uttered slanderous and libelous accusations at Slaton, he also directed some of his fury at Mrs. Slaton.

Leo Frank began serving his life sentence on June 22, 1915, at the Milledgeville Prison Farm, sometimes called the Georgia Penitentiary. He was assigned to work in the fields. On July 17 a twice- convicted murderer, William Creen stole a knife from the prison kitchen and crept into the cell where Frank lay sleeping. Creen slit Frank's throat from ear to ear. Only Frank's efforts to protect himself and the shouts of the other prisoners saved his life.

After the assault on Frank, Tom Watson resumed his vitriolic newspaper articles against Frank's commuted sentence. Many who read the articles became incensed once again, and called for Creen to be pardoned and released from prison.

When Governor Slaton commuted Leo Frank's sentence, a group who called themselves the Knights of Mary Phagan met at the young girl's grave in Marietta and pledged that they would avenge her death. Twenty-five men agreed that Frank would hang, and that they would share any consequences for the action they planned on taking. On the afternoon of August 16, the Knights of Mary Phagan set out for Milledgeville in eight cars, one by one. They convened in a field outside the prison.

Of the twenty-five, three of the men were masked. The others corned to hide their faces. With military precision, they broke through the prison gates and split into groups, each of which had specific objectives. One group cut the telephone lines and emptied the gasoline from the prison cars; another invaded the warden's home and handcuffed Warden Smith. A third group took over the Superintendent's office and handcuffed the Superintendent; while the fourth group went directly to Frank's cell where they handcuffed him and dragged him out to a waiting car. In a field just outside Marietta, Leo Frank was lynched in a grove of trees. When word of his death became known, hordes of people rushed to the grove to view Frank's body. No carnival ever attracted such a crowd. A Negro undertaker in Marietta arrived at the scene, and loaded the body into a wagon. Some of the spectators cut the rope from Frank's neck, chopped it into pieces and distributed it as souvenirs to the spectators.

The body was taken to the Greenberg and Bond Funeral Home in Atlanta. The funeral home admitted the public to the viewing of the body on August 17, and the throngs of people that lined up to view the body exceeded those who had viewed Mary Phagan's body. Leo Frank' remains were shipped to Brooklyn, New York, where they were buried in Cypress Hills in the Mount Carmel Cemetery.

Mary Phagan's Grave

215

The lynching of Leo Frank by a vigilante group had a profound effect on Georgia. On Thanksgiving Day, just two months after Frank's death, the Knights of Mary Phagan burned a huge cross on the top of Stone Mountain, and in doing so resurrected the defunct Klan. The Attorney General of the United States took steps to prosecute Tom Watson for his inflammatory articles on Leo Frank. He wanted to ban *The Jeffersonian* from the mails and initiate federal charges against Watson. Watson appealed to Governor Harris to intercede on his behalf and the case was dropped. The Knights of the Ku Klux Klan began a ten-year reign of terror, not only in the Southern states, but also in Indiana, New Jersey, Illinois, and to a lesser extent in some of the other northern states. Harry Golden quoted C. Vann Woodward in his biography of Watson as saying, "Yet if any mortal man may be credited (as no man may rightly be) with releasing the forces of human malice and ignorance and prejudice, which the Klan merely mobilized, that man was Thomas E. Watson." The vituperous articles Watson published in *The Jeffersonian* unleashed a mob mentality. It was not one of Georgia's finest moments to say the least.

Cursed Be This Town

Jacksonborough, Georgia, located midway between Augusta and Savannah on Beaver Dam Creek, was the county seat for Screven County, which had been formed in 1793.

Prior to the widespread cultivation of cotton, many of the farms in this part of the state were planted in tobacco. Georgia laws required that the tobacco be officially inspected and stamped with an inspector's mark before it could be exported. Public warehouses were located in a number of small towns, and it was in these that the tobacco was inspected and stamped, fees were paid, and the crop then exported to foreign markets via Savannah. Jacksonborough was one of the locations of the public warehouses. While this fact served to attract many people in the surrounding areas of the state, with the advent of the cotton gin and the subsequent popularity of cotton as a primary cash crop, Jacksonborough, like many similar small towns, was soon deprived of its economic importance.

The small town, aside from its role as the seat of government for the county, had little to commend itself as an urban city, but its taverns and saloons earned it a reputation as a wild frontier town. According to one source, it was noted that in the mornings after a particularly bad night of drunken brawls and fighting by the frontiersmen, children with teacups could be seen scooping up gouged eyeballs lying in the streets.

America in the early 1800s experienced a great religious revival a movement that spawned any number of religious groups and individuals who leaned heavily on the Old Testament for their sermons. Traveling across the country these revivalists set up church meetings in the towns for their pulpits. These revivals were characterized by their loud singing, praying, and exhortations on the evils of sin, and lengthy, forceful sermons that called sinners to repent their sinful ways. Worshippers would often immerse themselves in great frenzies of shouting, shaking, and speaking in tongues.

Lorenzo Dow was born in 1777 in Coventry, Connecticut, to Humphrey Dean Dow and his wife, Tabitha Parker Dow. The Dows were poor farmers who raised their son in the Congregationalist Church of New England, following a strong Calvinist traditional belief in predestination and original sin.

Young Lorenzo however, experienced soul-searching dreams and visions, and at one point in his young life contemplated suicide. In 1794, he made a decision to preach the gospel, but his first public preaching was not well received. Two years later, at the age of nineteen, Lorenzo Dow obtained a license to preach from the Method Church left home to become an itinerant evangelist. Although never ordained in the Methodist Church, he nonetheless spent a number of years traveling both to Great Britain and throughout America preaching in various towns. In 1804, he married Peggy Holcomb and had one child, a daughter who died in infancy.

Dow is described in various accounts as being a tall thin man with a fragile quality about him. His hair was long and straggly, and he was stoop-shouldered. His clothes were usually dark and dirty, and his general demeanor was unkempt. He was not above using tricks in order to gain converts to his impassioned way of interpreting Scripture. He earned the sobriquet "Crazy Dow."

It was the spring of 1821 when the renowned Rev. Dow arrived in the brawling frontier town of Jacksonborough, Georgia. Famous for his fire-and-brimstone sermons, he was offered lodging at the home of Seaborn Goodall, the Clerk of Court for Screven County and one of the few religious leaders in the town. It was arranged for Dow to speak at the Methodist

Church that evening, so Dow spent the day passing out handbills regarding the evening service.

The ringing of the church bell called the faithful to the service. Shortly after the opening hymns, some drunkards and troublemakers in the town gathered outside the church and began throwing rocks, shouting, and firing guns. The clatter and racket forced the meeting to break up, and the congregation left and returned to their homes.

The troublemakers and drunken rowdies returned to the saloons to continue their drinking.

The Rev. Dow was furious at the unexpected turn of events and grabbing an iron rod in his hand, he stormed into a saloon and smashed one of the whiskey barrels there. The incensed saloon patrons pinned Dow to the floor, and only the timely arrival of Seaborn Goodall on the scene rescued Dow from certain harm. Goodall took Dow to his home and treated his wounds.

The next morning the subdued Dow started out of town. Several of the instigators of the brawl the previous evening stopped Dow. Comments were directed at Dow concerning his slightly hunched back. The hoodlums proceeded to try the correct the hunchback by pressing him between two wide boards and sitting on him. Upon his release from this final indignity, an enraged Dow left Jacksonborough.

When he reached the bridge over Beaver Dam Creek, Dow paused and turned around, facing the frontier and stomped the dust of Jacksonborough from his feet. In a loud voice that rang through the small town, Dow cursed Jacksonborough and called down God's wrath to destroy the town, sparing only the house of Seaborn Goodall.

For the next twenty-five years, the gradual decline of the cursed town was helped along by storms, fires, and the other ravages of time. The population dwindled, and finally, in December of 1847, a new town and county seat was established five miles away at what is now Sylvania.

All that remains of Jacksonborough today is the forlorn Seaborn Goodall house that was built in 1815. It stands as the lone sentinel of a village long vanished. Only fields, woods, and a few dirt roads remain of what was once a thriving town.

Perhaps it is appropriate to note here that Jacksonborough was not the only Georgia town upon which a curse was placed. In 1820, John M. Harney, a weekly newspaper publisher in Savannah, had suffered devastating setbacks in his business. The weekly paper was not very popular and circulation of it declined. No doubt, the yellow fever epidemic contributed to his business' decline. Harney became quite bitter over the failure of his newspaper, and left Savannah and went to Charleston. Shortly before leaving Savannah, Harney wrote this in the final edition of his paper:

I leave you, Savannah, a curse that is far the worst of all curses – to remain as you are!

Although Savannah has moved into the 21st Century gracefully, the city has retained much of its 18th century ambience, a fact attested to by the number of tourists who visit the city each year to experience the authenticity of its large historic district. History literally seeps from its cobblestone ramps to the river and the moss-draped streets and squares. The curse, "to remain as you are," has created an economic boom never visualized by Harney. Harney himself did not fare too well after his departure from Savannah. From a brief stay in Charleston, he then moved to Kentucky. He died there in Kentucky a few years later.

South of the Border

Marlboro County, South Carolina, is in the northeast part of the state, just over the state line from Scotland County, North Carolina. Its close proximity to Laurinburg meant that the residents in either state shared a common heritage as well as other things. It is the largest county in South Carolina in area, covering nearly five hundred square miles, and is primarily agricultural with cotton as the predominant crop. Bennettsville is the county seat. Much of Marlborough County's population, at least in the northeastern part, was of Scottish descent.

As a child, I always thought of South Carolina as a place where antique shops were open on Sunday afternoons, a fact that did not escape my antique-loving mother. My brother and I spent many Sunday afternoons examining the treasures to be found in the dusty old homes that had been converted to the antique trade. We knew as much about Marlboro County and we did about our native Scotland County. The nearest South Carolina town of any size was Bennettsville, a town that had been founded in the late 1700s, though it was originally located a few miles south of the present day town. South of Bennettsville, U. S. Highway 15-401 South wound through farmland and crossed the Pee Dee River and passed through Society Hill, another Revolutionary town, and on toward Bishopville. I mention these towns because they were all on our Sunday itinerary. It was on these antiquing jaunts that my mother took the opportunity to relate the local history. As the on-site history lessons were usually repeated on each trip, we were soon fairly well versed in South Carolina lore about this area of the state.

Some of the stories of this area are unforgettable and bear repeating. My mother's versions did not always agree with some published accounts, but the history and the lessons she instilled were pretty much in agreement with other local versions. We probably knew as much of these events as some of the native families in the area.

We were very familiar with the exploits of Francis Marion, a.k.a. The Swamp Fox.

We read all of the historical markers dotted along the highways as well. It was one of these that introduced us to Colonel Kolb.

A Forgotten Grave

One particular site that we often visited was the lonely grave on the north side of the Pee Dee near a very old settlement known as Welsh Neck. An historical marker stands beside the highway. A small obelisk marks the grave in a small clearing on the bank of the Pee Dee. This is the grave of Revolutionary War patriot, Colonel Abel Kolb. The site today is littered with broken bottles, beer cans, and other trash. The obelisk itself has been damaged and defaced by vandals. The desolate location invites such sacrilege.

According to available accounts, the Kolb family arrived in the Marlboro area about 1751 and settled along the eastern shore of the Pee Dee River in a section called Welsh Neck. A Peter Kolb married Ann James, who was the daughter of the Rev. Philip James, minister of the Welsh Neck church. One of the children from this marriage was Abel Kolb, a man who would eventually be distinguished by his valuable Revolutionary War service to the patriots' cause. This service would include his death at the hand of Tory soldiers.

It was April 27, 1781, and as was true with so many parts of the country during the Revolutionary War, the Pee Dee River area was infiltrated with small contingents of British Redcoats and Tories. Col. Abel Kolb and his command of local militia were charged with the task of clearing the area of these Tories.

Kolb's militia had just returned to the Pee Dee after avenging the death of a young Whig by the name of Harry Sparks. Historians relate that some Tories had a hidden camp in the swamps near Blenheim. It was from this hideaway that they raided the countryside, pillaging, looting, and burning homes. Kolb and his men were looking for the camp to destroy it and run the Tories out. Young Harry Sparks volunteered to go into the swamp and try to locate the Tory camp.

When Sparks failed to return, Kolb's men entered the swamp, and in a clearing, discovered the corpse of Sparks hanging from a tree limb. Vowing revenge, Kolb's men pursued the fleeing Tories as far as what is today the North Carolina state line where they captured the fleeing British. Having confessed to the murder of Sparks, the guilty Tory was summarily executed by hanging.

Kolb returned to Welsh Neck, dismissed his men, and rode for home, anticipating a restful night's sleep. Unfortunately, for Kolb, that desire would not be fulfilled. In the early hours of the morning of April 28th, a group of vengeful Tories surrounded Kolb's house near the riverbank. Although Kolb's house was well built and could withstand enemy musket fire, the Tories set fire to the house. Col. Kolb, knowing that he was the target of the assault and wishing to protect his wife and daughters staying in the house, offered to surrender himself as a prisoner of war. The Tories accepted the terms of the surrender, but when Kolb stepped outside his doorway with his wife and daughters to surrender, a treacherous Tory fired a shot from his musket and Col. Kolb dropped dead at the doorway at the feet of his family. The Tories plundered the house and left it in flames when they hurriedly departed. The weeping wife and family dragged Kolb's body into the yard, away from the devouring flames.

This ignominious act was compounded when the raiding Tories surprised and killed a well-known Whig living the area and killed him, and then moved on to an old military prison where some British prisoners were being held. They released the two prisoners held there. The freed prisoners quickly moved on to plunder the house of a widow who reportedly had a secret stash of coins. After violently robbing her, they continued their way through the swamps and woodlands.

An old shoemaker named Willis was living on a meager patch of land where he had a small garden. He was usually ignored by the British as his age, poverty, and seeming neutrality, made him of little value to them. His only valuable possession was an old long fowling piece, which hung over his mantle. Having no doubt seen the smoke from Kolb's burning house and having heard the shots, he pulled down the gun, and when the Tories appeared neared his house, fired the gun bringing down both Tories who were dead in the road. He recovered the stolen money and returned it to the widow.

Col. Abel Kolb was buried near the spot where he fell. In 1973, The Marlboro County Historic Preservation Commission raised an obelisk over his grave. The inscription on the obelisk that guards his resting place reads:

A brave and Noble Soldier of the Era of '76
Lurking Tories failing to decoy him
From his house Which Stood Near the Ferry
Set fire to it
And in escaping From the Flames
He was shot
Ready as he was To Devote his all to His Country's Cause
He lost not sight of his Obligations to his God
He was a Worthy Member of the Welsh Neck Church
A long line of Admiring Descendants and Friends will Cherish
his Memory
With Profound Veneration.

Today an historical marker stands on Highway 15-4 01 near the State Road 167 that leads to Welsh Neck. It commemorates the death of Col. Abel Kolb. His home site is just off Highway 401 between the river and State Road 167. This is perhaps one of South Carolina's most forgotten and most neglected historical sites. It is not well kept, and trash covers much of the spot, which is apparently an ideal spot to fish in the river or to launch a small boat. Its remoteness lends a rather eerie atmosphere to the spot. It is not surprising that there are those who claim to see the figure of a man who comes through the woods at night. It stands first near the site of the old Kolb house, and then moves toward the riverbank where it gazes across the Pee Dee River from the spot where the old ferry once stood.

Col. Kolb's Grave

The Lady in the Woods

A small country cemetery, set back from a small modern brick church, and deep in the pinewoods is one of the few remaining landmarks of the small South Carolina community in Marlboro County known as Fletcher. For one blessed with a fertile imagination, a foggy morning or a late afternoon as the sun is setting, can call up images of the past. The silence can be quite eerie.

It is not a great leap to visualize a lone visitor coming through the woods in the dark, threading his way among the old tombstones scattered among the tree. Suddenly, he is confronted by the life-size figure of a lady stepping down from one of the stones. He halts in startled confusion, his first and immediate inclination to turn and flee through the woods to the surrounding open fields.

The Fletcher family, a prominent and quite prosperous family has a long history in Marlboro County. Anna Cedelle Fletcher, the daughter of John C. and Bettie Ann Gibson Fletcher, was born December 19, 1893. She died at the age of 31, and like so many who die young, romantic legends have sprung up to explain Anna Cedelle's early death and the incredibly lovely marble statue that guards her grave. Several versions of the legend exist, but most agree that Anna Cedelle, as she was called by family and friends, graduated from Columbia College and returned home where she fell in love with a young medical doctor, Everett Livingston of Gibson, North Carolina. They had been friends while she was in college. They were engaged to be married, but as fate would have it, this was not to be. Anna Cedelle became ill with a mysterious malady. She grew weak and eventually withdrew to her home, seldom venturing out.

There are those who suggest that Anna Cedelle's decline was due in part to her grieving over the death of a cousin, Robert T. Fletcher, who died October 7, 1918, shortly before Armistice was declared, in Meuse-Argonne, France, during the first World War. She and Robert were close kin, being double first cousins, in fact. His death in battle was a blow to the family, and Anna Cedelle must have been intensely affected by it. Both had grown up together as part of the tight-knit Fletcher family.

As Anna Cedelle's health became increasingly worse, she broke off her engagement with young Dr. Livingston. The Fletcher family, being quite affluent, took her to several doctors and even brought a doctor down from Philadelphia to examine their daughter. Although she received the best medical care available at that time, her illness became increasingly worse.

Finally, on February 22, 1925, Anna Cedelle Fletcher died and was laid to rest in the little country cemetery behind Fletcher Wesleyan Church in Marlboro County, South Carolina, in the same cemetery where her cousin Robert had been buried in 1918.

It is at this point that romanticists embellish the story of the statue, attributing its presence to grief-stricken Dr. Livingston who commissioned it, using a picture of Anna Cedelle as the model. However, the most commonly held version, which the Fletcher family verifies, is that John C. Fletcher sent a photograph of Anna Cedelle to a sculptor in Italy. There a slightly larger-than-life size statue was carved in Italian marble, using the photograph as a model, at a cost of $10,000. The completed statue was shipped to Fletcher, South Carolina, where it was installed descending the granite steps of Anna Cedelle's monument.

Grave of Anna Cedelle Fletcher

It is interesting to note, that Anna Cedelle's fiancé, Dr. Livingston never married. Perhaps he never recovered from Anna Cedelle's premature death. He died in 1959 and was buried beside his parents in the Gibson Cemetery.

There in the quiet woods off Highway 381 in Marlboro

County, frozen in time, the statue of the lovely Anna Cedelle Fletcher seems to be stepping down from the granite monument that marks her grave. Although the statue has become a victim to the ravages of time and weather, broken fingers and chipped places, it is still a beautiful tribute to a young woman.

Things That Go Bump in the Night

It was late June of 1988, and Christopher Davis, then seventeen years old, had just finished changing a flat tire on his car. It was 2:00 a.m., and Chris, who had worked the late shift at McDonald's, was on his way home when his tire went flat near Scape Ore Swamp on the outskirts of the small town of Bishopville, South Carolina, a town of about 3,500 people in 1988.

He wearily placed the tire jack into the trunk of the car, a 1976 Celica Toyota, when he observed a very large creature running toward him from a nearby field. Jumping quickly into the car, Chris tried to slam the door closed, but the creature grabbed the side mirror on the door and tried to pull the door open. Having frantically started the engine, Chris accelerated sharply, but his attacker managed to jump on top of the car. According to young Chris, the creature, which walked on its hind legs, stood over seven feet tall, had red eyes that appeared to glow, and was covered with scaly green skin. Its hands and feet had three fingers or toes each, and each had a four-inch black talon at its tip. The sudden acceleration and the speed with which Chris sped away caused the reptile-like creature to fall off.

Upon arriving at home after his terrifying ordeal, Chris, panic-stricken, woke his parents and related what had occurred. He was obviously in a state of shock. Chris' father examined the car and found that the mirror was twisted and hanging from the door of the car. The top of the car showed deep gouges and scratches. Something out of the ordinary had certainly taken place. Mr. Davis reasoned that the matter was best handled by police, and he duly notified the authorities.

Liston Truesdale was the sheriff of Lee County, and it was his department that responded to the call from Mr. Davis. The authorities concurred that Chris had certainly seen something that night, but they had no clue as to what it might have been. In the days that followed this incident, the sheriff's department received numerous calls from uneasy townspeople who heard odd sounds or noises at night, and whose dogs and farm animals appeared to act strangely. Deputies made casts of large three-toed tracks, which were purportedly made by the "Lizard Man," as the creature was dubbed. A wildlife biologist examined the tracks and pronounced them man-made. One reported sighting came from a man who was driving along nearby Interstate 20 and spotted the reptilian creature. He took a shot at it and believed that he had hit it. As proof, he offered some bloody scales. A quick look at this evidence by authorities identified the scales as coming from a fish, but the blood and scales were sent to the state crime lab for analysis and confirmation. Another report came from a young couple who stated that Lizard Man had pulled the chrome and molding off their car while they were parked at a lovers' lane in the same vicinity. Hundreds of people and reporters converged on Bishopville, hoping to glimpse the Lizard Man. Manhunts to find the elusive creature were organized by some locals. These posses searched the nearby swamps for signs of the creature. Many people wrote the whole thing off as an elaborate hoax. One member of the local law enforcement office suggested that Davis might have seen a bear, which had come to a nearby artesian spring to drink. There was no doubt that Chris had seen something, but no one could come up with a reasonable explanation.

Almost overnight, the little backwater town of Bishopville had become a destination for curiosity seekers. Locals were quick to capitalize on the publicity, well aware that fame is fleeting. T-shirts, caps, inflatable lizards, bumper stickers, and posters depicting a reptilian creature based on Chris Davis' description flooded the town.

Other reports of sightings or encounters with the elusive lizard man came into the sheriff's office. Each one was faithfully investigated with disappointing or inconclusive results. Sheriff Truesdale announced that each person who reported a sighting would be asked to submit to a polygraph.

Indeed, Chris Davis himself was administered a polygraph by Sumter Police Captain Earl Berry on August 18, 1988. The results of that test were not released to the public.

Sheriff Truesdale did admit that his office had received a report that another resident had mentioned to a deputy that he had seen a similar creature the previous fall while he was hunting in the swamp.

Another witness, a thirty-one year old construction worker told authorities that the previous fall he had been riding his bike home sometime after midnight and had stopped at the artesian well for a drink of water and to smoke a cigarette. He spotted something on the other side of the road, and at first assumed he was looking at a dead tree. When the thing moved, he observed that it was seven or eight feet tall, standing upright on two legs. A car passed by on the road and the headlights of the car reflected the red eyes of the creature, which then turned and went back into the swamp. The witness said that he thought he was seeing a "haint," or ghost. When he told his family, his brother did not believe him and thought he was crazy.

By late August, reports of sightings died down, and only a few instances of the appearance of the Lizard Man were reported. Since that June night, there have been occasional reports of someone spotting the lizard-like creature, but the excitement generated by Chris Davis' experience finally quieted down altogether.

This strange tale has its counterparts in other areas of the country. It may be just another version or adaptation of an urban legend that made its way to Lee County, South Carolina. No one can say for sure. The furor died down for lack of new information or reports, but there has never been a credible explanation for what Davis saw that lonely night, nor has any tangible evidence of this reptilian creature surfaced to dispel any doubts of its existence.

As a brief historical footnote to this story, it may be of interest to the reader to learn the origin of the name, Scape Ore Swamp. Although there are some who think the name has some reference to mining, most local historians believe that the name Scape Ore is a euphemism for Escaped Whore, a name based on an event that occurred during the Revolutionary War period in this area.

According to these experts, it seems that a small group of British redcoats had camped on a small island in the swamp. Accompanying this troop were several female camp followers, or whores. This was a common occurrence during wars. A local patriot, by the name Redden McCoy, gathered a small group of local militia to drive the British out of the swamp. The militia entered the swamp and was apparently heard by the whores, who quickly fled the camp. By doing so, these ladies of the night escaped capture by the local militia. Locals who were familiar with the historical significance of the swamp named the swamp Escaped Whore Swamp. Eventually, this colorful name was corrupted to Scape Ore, thus "cleaning up" a name that they felt was far too explicit for innocent young ears.

S.O.B., or That Tacky Tourist Trap

No account of the lower Pee Dee area would be complete without at least a passing mention of that oddity on Highway 301 South known as South of the Border, or just as S.O.B. by locals. It is situated just south of the North Carolina state line, hence its name. The history of this sprawling complex of shops, restaurants, and rooms is one of those rags to riches story. It had its humble beginnings as a small beer stand that offered refreshments to travelers heading south. It also sold firecrackers, the sales of which were illegal in North Carolina. Lewis Grizzard, that earthy and beloved columnist of the *Atlanta Journal and Constitution*, once referred to South of the Border as "the Yankee Immigration Station." The founder of this tacky tourist Mecca was a thirty-six year old entrepreneur by the name of Alan Heller Schafer.

According to most accounts, Schafer was born into a Jewish family in Baltimore in 1914. While still a very young child, his family moved to the outskirts of Dillon, South Carolina. Abraham Schafer, father of Samuel Schafer and grandfather of Alan Schafer, had operated a general merchandise business in Little Rock, South Carolina, since the Reconstruction era. Abraham died during the Great Depression. His son, Samuel, was involved in the store as well. Samuel's son, Alan, at that time was a student at the University of South Carolina majoring in journalism. He left school and came home to help the family sell the business. Samuel and Alan began a wholesale beer distributorship with two trucks.

U.S. Highway 301 was a major route for the many families

who traveled to the South Carolina beaches and also Northern travelers on their way to Florida. A "Bubba" character was created to help sell the soft drink. Showing political acumen, "Bubba" also became a staunch advocate for the Democratic party By the time Interstate 95 was developed, Schafer had acquired enough political power for the highway to take a little jog that would take it through South of the Border. Indeed, throughout his lifetime, Schafer rose to become a powerbroker whose influence was felt across South Carolina.

Alan's abilities in the management field enabled the Schafers to expand the business. They also branched out into other commercial ventures, the most important of which became the construction of a complex of businesses. It was there that the concept of actually creating a new town designed with the northern tourist in mind was born. Schafer was extremely creative, and the logo he designed was that of a jolly little Mexican in a huge sombrero named Pedro. In the late 1950s, the restaurant at South of the Border became the place for teenagers to have dinner after local high school proms.

The character Pedro very quickly became a familiar figure in the advertisements and flamboyant billboards for South of the Border. Soon his cheerful countenance, quoting clever sayings, began to appear on large billboards all along U. S. Highway 301, and later on Interstate 95. These quotes, while not usually rhyming, are somewhat reminiscent of the old Burma Shave signs that once dotted the nation's highways.

Today, South of the Border is undoubtedly the largest source of employment for Dillon County. Originally a small retail beverage stand on Highway 301 which catered mainly to tourist traffic going to and from Florida and also the Myrtle Beach traffic, the huge complex, consisting of restaurants, motels, golf course, zoo, tennis courts, amusement park, and miniature railroad, that is South of the Border today does not have an exact counterpart anywhere in the United States. Wall Drug Store in South Dakota may come close.

While the ideas and concepts of his famous billboards originated with Schafer, he eventually hired public relations experts to carry out his ideas. Countless children traveling with their parents watched avidly for a glimpse of the next South of the Border sign. Who can resist such clever billboard exhortations as:

"Fill Up Your Trunque Weeth Pedro's Junque!" or
"Keep Yelling, Kids! They'll Stop." or
"Weather forecast – Hot today. Chili tamale"?

Schafer's entrepreneurial instincts led him to purchase Blenheim Ginger Ale in the early 1990s. This beverage with its spicy bite was concocted in Blenheim, South Carolina, and was once used for colds or nasal congestion. Know that while Georgia had its Coca Cola and North Carolina its Pepsi Cola, Schafer wanted Blenheim Ginger Ale to take its place in the history of South Carolina. While Blenheim Ginger Ale continues to be bottled and sold locally, it has never achieved the distinction enjoyed by either Coca Cola or Pepsi Cola.

Nevertheless, Schafer's business acumen, luck, genial personality, and golden touch were not enough to earn him immunity from a federal lawsuit. In 1981, Alan Schafer was convicted in a federal vote buying scandal. He served a year's sentence in federal prison.

He spent large sums of money in campaigns to promote video gambling. Until the South Carolina outlawed video games, South of the Border's Silver Slipper operated the largest video gambling operation in South Carolina. In an ensuing lawsuit brought by former South Carolina governor David Beasley's campaign against Schafer and another gambling entrepreneur, Fred Collins, Circuit Judge Tom Ervin ruled in favor of Schafer and Collins.

In 1993, Schafer once again made the news when he received a complaint from the Mexican Embassy protesting his depiction of Mexicans through the character of Pedro that appeared on South of the Border's billboards. Unperturbed by such official protest, Schafer replied to the Mexican Embassy in a letter which highlighted the fact that South of the Border spent more than $1.5 dollars a year in the importation of Mexican merchandise which was then sold in the shops. Money often speaks louder than words, and in this instance, the complaint seems to have died a natural death. The friendly, smiling Pedro still adorns some of the billboards.

The often controversial, but always flamboyant, Alan Schafer died of leukemia on July 19, 2001. He was 87. He had the distinction of being the most successful businessman in the country, and perhaps, in the world at that time.

South of the Border still continues to exercise its glitzy charm on the thousands of tourists who travel I-95. For some it is a tradition to stop and take in all of the tourist trap paraphernalia for which SOB is widely known. Newer tourists succumb to the superb advertising billboards that seduce the eye, especially the eye of the younger ones to stop and enjoy the many attractions offered at SOB. Schafer may be gone, but his advertising genius lives on in the colorful billboards, the 97-foot high Pedro, the giant trademark 207-foot high sombrero, and the empire he created.

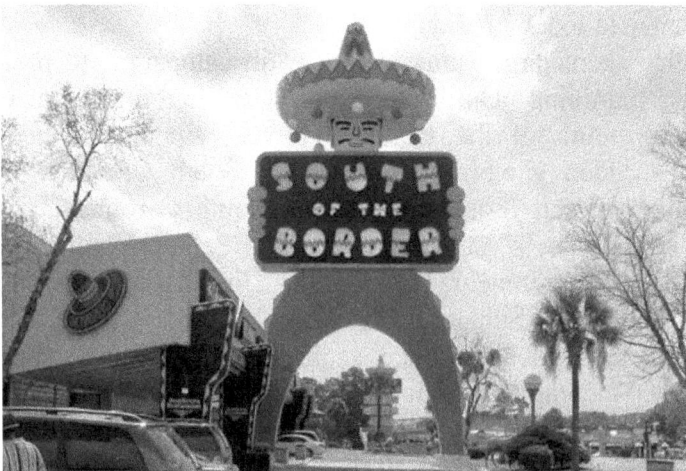

Those Mysterious Booms

A book of this nature would be incomplete if it did not include brief mention of that unique phenomenon known in some parts of the country as the "Seneca Guns," so-called after Seneca Lake, New York, where they have been heard since the 1800s. There are those who call them "sky quakes," believing that the sounds originate when hot and cold air masses come together suddenly in the upper atmosphere. Meteorologists have yet to discover the source of the boomings, and other scientists have suggested that they are caused by large bubbles of gas rising to the surface of bodies of water. Other explanations have been proffered as well, but none of them seem to solve the mystery.

This mysterious booming has been heard periodically, not only in Seneca, New York, but also in parts of South Carolina, and more recently in North Carolina, particularly along the Wilmington coastal area. While usually heard in areas where there are large bodies of water, apparently they are not confined to such areas.

Once while traveling north on Interstate 20 towards Cheraw, South Carolina, my husband and I stopped to buy peaches at a roadside stand near the small town of McBee. After purchasing the peaches and returning to our car, we were startled to hear extremely loud booms that shook the ground. The sound was that of a cannon being fired. We searched the sky, thinking at first that we were hearing sonic booms from jets flying overhead, but soon realized that was not the case. Nor were we near any military installation that might be firing large guns on a firing range. We even considered the possibility of an earthquake and thought of tectonic plates under intense pressure deep in the earth rubbing against or colliding with one another. None of these explanations fit, however, and the owner of the roadside peach stand commented that those booms are heard periodically, but no one seems to know where or how they originate.

Science still has no concrete explanation for the mysterious booms heard periodically in various places, both at home and abroad. It is only fitting that the South share in the bounty. With all apologies to Mr. Shakespeare, there are more things in heaven than dreamed of in our scientific philosophies, Horatio.

Stars and Bars

I would be remiss if I did not comment on that one topic that seems to bring out the worst in many people, particularly those whose knowledge of history is stunted by prejudice, or just plain ignorance of historical facts. Some people have a tendency to suffer paroxysms of anger over anything that mentions the word "Confederate." They are those who want to brush off that portion of our nation's history as if it never existed. Well, folks, unfortunately the years 1861-1865 did exist and you can never wipe them out. Confederate flags did fly over the South, and they are honorable flags indeed. The men who fought under those flags were not monsters; they were honorable men defending their homeland. Their descendants continue to serve their country today. Some were good; some were not. A nation cannot in good conscience erase its history, nor can it ignore it. To do so is to jeopardize the very tenets on which our nation was founded. Racism takes many forms, and an agenda to erase those parts of history one does not like, or to destroy those symbols that extol that history is censorship of the worst kind. It is a basic freedom to honor those who gave their lives for a cause they believed in. Soldiers do this today on every battlefield in the world, often for causes that are not just or that are not popular. Shall we condemn them also?

The issue of Confederate flags becomes a political football all too often. Yet, those who fear it do not realize that not a single Confederate flag ever flew on a slave ship. Contrary to the prevailing misconception, the Confederate flag was never used by the Ku Klux Klan in the early part of the 20th Century. In fact, photographs of 1920s Klan rallies and processions show the American flag being carried. Those who argue the loudest know the least. Too many misconceptions and myths have been perpetuated as history. History is written by the victors, but this does not make it complete or even necessarily true, but then everyone is a self-styled expert. We see this today in the conflicts and wars that are conducted on foreign soil. The history is made to fit political agendas and to justify political actions. After all, the reasons for the War Between the States in the first place are so complex and so misunderstood, that it takes a political scholar to try to make sense of it all. It cannot be simplified by saying that the war was fought over slavery. This makes as much sense as saying that the war in Iraq was fought over September 11th. Behind every declaration of war by any nation against another is a complex tangle of political maneuverings for power and wealth. War is declared by the few, but it is fought by the average soldier who follows the orders of his leaders. Not a single Southerner living today would endorse slavery, but neither is he going to disclaim or condemn his ancestors. Those are family, and that was a different era. He is not going to forget that those ancestors lived and died for their beliefs. Many Southerners may be prejudiced, but that is very different from being racist.

One of the fascinating bits in all of this is the fact that those people who decry any public display of what they call the "Stars and Bars" do not, in fact, know what the "Stars and Bars" really looks like. This is where ignorance rears its ugly head. The name is blindly applied the name to the Confederate Battle flag, under the mistaken belief that the two names are synonymous. They are not the same, and they do not refer to the same flag at all. There were actually five different official Confederate flags, in addition to those created and used by various regiments and units.

The Stars and Bars is also known as the First National Flag

of the Confederacy. It was adopted March 14, 1861, and consisted of two horizontal red bars separated by a white bar. A dark blue field in the upper left corner contained seven stars, a number which changed to thirteen later.

Following this, in May of 1863, the Second National Flag was adopted. This flag was all white except for a red field with the St. Andrew's cross in the upper left corner. Its first official use was to drape the coffin of Stonewall Jackson, thus earning it the name "Jackson Flag" or "The Stainless Banner." This was not used long because, in the heat of the battlefield, it was sometimes mistaken for a flag of truce.

The Third National Flag was adopted March 4, 1865. It was almost identical to the Second National Flag, but a vertical red bar had been added. This flag was only used a very short time because when it was officially adopted, the end of the war was only weeks away.

The Battle Flag, a red flag with a blue St. Andrew's cross, which contained the twelve stars of the Confederate States, was originally designed as a Confederate Naval jack and was square. The St. Andrew's cross recalls the Scots-Irish ancestry of the Southern people.

And then there was a fifth flag used by the Confederacy, but it was never an officially adopted. That was the Bonnie Blue Flag, a solid dark blue flag with a single white star in the center. This flag has a very long history dating to 1810 when it was adopted as the flag of the very short-lived Republic of West Florida. It served as a model for the flag of Texas, which fought under this flag in 1835. The Texas flag used a single yellow star on a blue field. When the Ordinance of Secession was read in Jackson, Mississippi, January 26, 1861, an Irish immigrant from Ulster was present for the occasion. He watched as the blue flag with a single white star was raised over the capitol building. The sight inspired him to write a song, "The Bonnie Blue Flag," a ballad that named the states of the Confederacy in order, popularized this flag.

The Bonnie Blue flag, though never officially adopted by the Confederacy, was embraced by the Southern people. The song by that title, written by Harry McCarthy, became the second most popular song in the Confederacy.

It is unfortunate that so many people do not understand the reverence that Southerners hold for their ancestors. While it is true that Lee surrendered at Appomattox Courthouse, that surrender does not mean that Southerners gave up their right to be Southern and their right to honor their forebears. This reverence extends to the various flags under which our Confederate ancestors fought and died.

A case in point is poignantly illustrated in very recent times at a Methodist church in coastal Georgia. This particular church dates to the 1850s, and during the War Between the States this church served as a hospital for Confederate soldiers who were stationed at the numerous batteries and camps that formed the coastal defenses in the area. Many of the men who were hospitalized here were not there due to battle wounds primarily, but were suffering from the many diseases such as malaria, dysentery, and other ailments that plagued both armies. In the small churchyard adjoining the church are the graves of 33 unknown Confederate soldiers who died in the church. An early chapter of the United Daughters of the Confederacy erected the familiar iron crosses that mark many Confederate throughout the South.

Since the year 2014 marks the 120th anniversary of the founding of the United Daughters of the Confederacy, the nation's oldest women's patriotic society, the local chapter of the UDC asked permission to hold a ceremony in the church on Confederate Memorial Day in April. At this ceremony, three United States veterans would be presented with the UDC's Military Service Awards. The medals to be awarded honored a World War II veteran, a Vietnam veteran, and a veteran of the Global War on Terror. During the ceremony, the American flag would be presented and the Pledge of Allegiance recited, followed by the singing of the National Anthem Following this, a salute to the First National Flag would also be recited, following by the singing of Dixie's Land. After the ceremony, the participants would move outside to the little cemetery and a bronze plaque honoring the 33 unknown Confederate soldiers buried there would be dedicated.

Permission was secured from the pastor of the church and also from the Board of Trustees of the church. Two week later, the chairman of the trustees called the UDC Chapter's President and told her that they were withdrawing permission to hold this ceremony at the church. He explained that there was a problem with some of the trustees of the church who were adamant that the "Stars and Bars "could not be used in the church. It seems that the trustees had second thoughts and were divided in their opinions. Those opposing the ceremony were individuals who had moved to this small coastal community from other parts of the country. They really had no concept of the history of the community in which they had made their homes. They came to this area because they wanted to live in the idyllic ambiance of the South, but they do not want the history of the South to intrude in their lives. There is an old Southern saying that is timeless in its meaning. "Just because you have silenced a man does not mean that you have converted him."

Major William Green

In later years, in my pursuit of family genealogy, I came across the story of a distant great grandfather, Major William Green. Had she known about him, my mother would have been delighted with this old scoundrel. He made a name for himself during the American Revolution, and then later in the North Carolina legislature. His career as a Revolutionary War soldier was somewhat checkered, however, and had a number of twists and turns before he finally got it all together and served honorably in the American war for independence.

Green became somewhat of a legend in North Carolina. Purported to be the first white child born on Buffalo Creek in what is today Cleveland County, William Green was the son of Joseph and Mary McIntyre Green. He was born May 16, 1753, and would become a historical figure of some note in the history of Rutherford County where he made his home.

William Green became a captain in the Tryon Militia in the early days of the Revolution. He was a staunch Whig at the time. When the British Army, under General Lord Cornwallis, landed at Charleston in April of 1780, it cut a swath across South Carolina and Georgia, and threatened North Carolina. Under orders from Cornwallis, Colonel Patrick Ferguson amassed about 4,000 Loyalists and subdued the small settlements in Rutherford County. The Tryon Militia, its numbers much reduced, retreated leaving the settlers to face the British. Captain William Green, who had been captured by Tories and who was freed only after the Battle of Ramseur's Mill, experienced an epiphany in regard to his personal political inclinations. He gathered a troop of militia and arrived at Col. Ferguson's camp in Rutherfordton where he offered his militia in support of the King.

Given a commission with the rank of Major, Green joined Ferguson's Tory forces and marched south to join Lord Cornwallis at Charlotte. In the meantime, however, the patriot troops marched across country and caught up with Ferguson's troops at King Mountain. In the ensuing Battle of King's Mountain, Col. Ferguson was killed, and the British troops, including Maj. Green, were captured. Along with several other officers, William Green was tried for treason and was sentenced to hang. Green and another officer managed to free themselves and fled into the wilds of Rutherford County. It is believed by some that Green's stepfather, James McAfee, aided him in eluding would-be captors. When Green failed to appear at the trial of other Tories for treason and other crimes, his property was confiscated.

While his motives may be questioned, William Green appeared before authorities, declared his Whig sympathies, and enlisted in the American army. He also managed to recover his confiscated property. This innate sense of self-preservation would seem to characterize Green's life. He served in the American army until the end of the Revolution and then settled down on his farm to raise a family. His desire for peaceful obscurity lasted fourteen years until 1798. That year William Green made a foray into state politics and won a seat in the North Carolina House of Representatives. Following this victory, he went on to be elected to the North Carolina Senate where he served fourteen terms in office.

In 1818, Green was opposed in his bid for re-election to the Senate. Displaying his usual political acumen, Senator Green made the decision to be baptized into the Baptist Church where he hoped to gather winning votes. The baptism was to be by immersion in the Broad River. This event drew a very large group of observers that included his opponent, Elias Alexander,

Jr. As Green was being raised from the waters, Alexander spoke out loudly with the following rhyme: "There stands old Major Green, now neat and clean, though formerly a Tory, the damnedest rascal that ever was seen, now on his way to Glory."

Nevertheless, Green's long tenure in the North Carolina Legislature was an honorable one. When he retired from politics, he lived with one of his sons until his death November 6, 1832. He was buried in the old Green family cemetery located near the old Bostic Brickyard. His son William, born in 1789, married Jane Baber in Rutherford County on October 29, 1817. They moved to Georgia and settled between Marietta and Dallas. One of William's sons, Napoleon Bonaparte Green, served as a Representative from Cobb County to the Confederate Legislature, thereby continuing the affinity of the Green family for political careers.

Gone to the Dogs

While dog lovers know no political boundaries and no geographical section of the country has a monopoly on the love of Man's best friend, the special place in their hearts that Southerners reserve for their canine companions is perhaps a reflection of their Celtic heritage. From the favorite hunting dogs of the country gentleman to the coonhounds of the farmer to the boudoirs shared with pampered pooches, these noble creatures exert an influence over our lives. Few indeed are the Southerners who cannot boast of owning at least one memorable and unforgettable dog in their lifetime.

Some of the foregoing stories have involved dogs in one sense or another. John and I have lived with our share, including our beloved little Silky Terrier named Cedric, who graciously allows us to share his home. It was our first dog as a married couple, however, that introduced us to the "paranormal" powers that some dogs are rumored to possess. While I have a tendency to scoff at the proliferation of supernatural or paranormal tales that seems to slip into so many facets of modern life, nevertheless, I must admit to experiencing some instances that seem to defy any explanation.

The occurrence that comes to mind as being most memorable, however, involved John's black standard poodle, Caesar. Caesar was born in the little community of Oceanway, Florida in 1963. At that time, John had become interested in dog shows, and it was not long before Caesar entered his first show, which happened to be a puppy match. Other AKC shows followed, and Caesar soon racked up quite a collection of blue ribbons and even a silver trophy. Although Caesar never earned his championship, John derived a great deal of pleasure in mingling with the doggy set that frequented the southeastern dog shows. When his show career ended, Caesar was bred once, and choosing to accept the pick of the litter in lieu of a stud fee, we acquired Tanya. Both dogs became an integral part of our lives, traveling everywhere with us.

In July of 1979, Tanya, who had become nearly blind in her later years, wandered into the path of a speeding car. We buried her in the backyard in Laurinburg, and then returned to our home in Harlem, Georgia. Caesar became extremely despondent after Tanya's death, and lost all interest in eating. He, like many dogs with long, floppy ears, had developed an ear infection that failed to respond to treatments. This condition included a distinctive odor from the waxy discharge, and while it was not extremely unpleasant, it was definitely unmistakable and recognizable.

On October 1979, John and I came home from work one afternoon, and as we unlocked our kitchen door, we spotted Caesar on the floor. The evening before, he had come into the bedroom and stood in the doorway staring at me, before returning to his bed. It was evident the next day that he had suffered heart failure and died there in the kitchen. Sadly, John dug a grave in our backyard and we wrapped Caesar in an old quilt and buried him. John had a small stone engraved with Caesar's picture and name, and this was placed on the grave.

With both dogs gone, it soon occurred to us that coming home to an empty house in the evening was rather depressing. We missed having a dog greet us with wagging tail. Not able to face another poodle, our next dog was a Silky Terrier named Sir Cedric Bang-Bang. His personality was quite different from that of the poodles. Once, in our apartment in Savannah, I missed Cedric. Hearing him bark in the hallway outside our door, I looked out in time to see him step off one of the elevators. I have no idea how long he had been gone, nor do I know where he went. My only question is who pushed the elevator button for him to return home?

In 1983, we moved from Harlem to the military town of Hinesville, Georgia It was soon after that move, that we began noticing on occasion the whiff of the ear infection that had plagued Caesar. It would suddenly become noticeable in the car when we were driving. Once, I caught a glimpse of a black poodle in our apartment in Hinesville and smelled that odor. We realized that Caesar was still with us and he was not particularly happy about being left behind in Harlem when we moved. These manifestations continued for several years.

We had rented out our house in Harlem, but after a year or two of dealing with renters, we decided to sell the house. We made an agreement with the buyer that we would move Caesar's grave. On Good Friday of 1985, we drove to Harlem and disinterred Caesar's remains, placed them in a small wooden box, and took him to Laurinburg.

There we buried him beside Tanya. From that day on, we never again smelled the ear odor, and we never again had a glimpse of Caesar. Today, he and Tanya rest in our little private pet cemetery, along with Miss Lil' Britches, a cat, and Sir Cedric Bang-Bang. Their graves are all marked, and they are all together.

We currently live with our second Silky, also named Cedric. Ceddie leads a charmed life. Once when he was not quite a year old, he slipped his collar while we were out for a walk and ran to get away from some children who began chasing him. I frantically searched the streets, but could not find him. Finally, I returned to our apartment to find that Ceddie had crossed Abercorn Street and Drayton Street, two of the busiest streets in Savannah. He made his way back to the DeRenne and went to each of the three doors trying to get in the building. A student picked him up and knocked on the door. A house cleaner in the building told the student which apartment was ours.

251

Ceddie once jumped on the elevator in our building and the door closed, trapping his leash. While John and I panicked, the second elevator door opened a minute or two later and Ceddie, minus his collar, stepped out. On another occasion, I had stopped at an intersection. As I turned the corner, Ceddie jumped out of the car and rolled under the moving car. Braking quickly, I jumped out, expecting to find his lifeless body lying in the street. Instead, I found him sniffing a bush on the side of the road. He has two best friends, Dixie Belle, a Pembroke Welsh Corgi, and Pikku, an Italian Greyhound. He has given us a great deal of pleasure, operating on the assumption that if you lick hands, and act cute, you can get away with anything. He gives unconditional love, and asks only to be with us every waking moment. He is the dog of our old age.

Pikku and Ceddie

Home at Last

It is sometimes a challenge to put together a book that incorporates so many different elements into its pages. All of the stories had some relevance to me at the time they were discovered or told to me. All of them have a special appeal. The individuals mentioned in this book earned their niche here, not because they were famous or because they did famous or heroic deeds, but because they were real people who just may have been a little half step off the beat of the drummer. Their joys, their sorrows, their triumphs, and their tragedies were theirs alone, yet they were all part of a whole. Their humanity made them important in their own little corner.

The oddities, the strange or sometimes mystifying tales are part and parcel of our everyday lives. These make up our heritage as surely as our beliefs and our genealogies. Those who live in the Southern low country have often been accused of adhering to an Oriental philosophy – we eat a lot of rice and we worship our ancestors. As blasphemous as this statement may appear on the surface, the truth is not that we worship our ancestors (Lord knows some of them were not particularly reputable or worthy of worship), but rather that we acknowledge them and their legacy to us. After all, if we don't know where we came from, how in heaven's name will we know where we are going? Our ancestors give us direction and purpose, and hopefully, it is a good direction and a good purpose. We are certainly not all good, but neither are we all bad. The important thing is establishing a balance, learning from past mistakes, and creating a better present and future.

Southerners do not live in the past, but neither do we care to forget it. If we are melancholy at times, it may be because we see too clearly and we are fearful of what may be lost and what may be exalted. We cannot stem the tide of progress, but perhaps we can slow some aspects of the less desirable innovations. The key is not to ever forget who we are.

These stories and anecdotes are part and parcel of our way of life. While they may not be especially unique to our beloved section of the nation, they do serve to represent those qualities common to all humanity – love of home and family, tragedy, and hope for the future. We carve our own place, and by doing so, we shape who we are. Old values are still worthwhile, and it is important to examine them on occasion just to make sure that we are still on track. These values, honesty, love, concern for others, and joy in simple pleasures never go out of date, although they are sometimes shoved on a back burner.

One sad postscript that I am now compelled to add is the death of our dear little Ceddie. He had been sick for several days and had lost most of his hair and most of his body mass. On September 7, 2011, at about 5:30 a.m., I awoke to find Ceddie lying on the floor beside the recliner where I had dozed off to sleep the previous evening. He was cold and weak, and I wrapped him in a small blanket and picked him up. He whimpered softly and I knew that I was going to lose my little buddy. Dr. Lester came to the house and I held Ceddie in my arms while Dr. Lester administered first a sedative and then the final injection. He was cremated and his ashes placed in a small carved wooden box. John and I agreed that whichever of us departed this life first, Ceddie's remains would be placed in the casket and thus rest with one of us always.

That time came sooner than either of us ever dreamed. After several years of failing health, my beloved John quietly passed away on January 6, 2012, as I sat by his bedside. His funeral was held at the Cathedral of St. John the Baptist in Savannah. In his hands was the tiny box with the ashes of

Ceddie. There was not a dry eye in the church when Monsignor William O'Neill, who conducted the service, mentioned that Ceddie was accompanying John on his final journey home.

With John's death in January, my life took a drastic turn. I had spent the last three years caring for John at home, and now he was gone, Ceddie was gone, and I was alone. After nearly fifty years of friendship, courtship and marriage how does one reconcile one's self to being alone?

This question had always bothered John and he knew that I would be left to deal with life after his demise. I had assured him many times that I would be all right. He was an astute financial manager and therefore, there were no concerns in that respect. He had made sure that I would be well-provided for, and we had no outstanding bills. I, on the other hand was an intensely private individual, somewhat of a loner, had numerous interests and hobbies, and had been used to handling the routine concerns of everyday life. Due to his illness, many things that he had undertaken were responsibilities that I had shouldered when the need arose. In retrospect, I am not sure that I always did things the way he would have, or even the best way, but I managed to get through, and would say a silent prayer that I had made good decisions.

John and I had led a fairly adventurous life after we had retired.

John and Ceddie

We had traveled extensively, both in the States and overseas, and we did the things we had always dreamed of doing. We went to Ireland and we kissed the Blarney stone, albeit at great risk to life and limb. We saw the pyramids at Giza and entered the Great Pyramid there. We actually were allowed to crawl into a sarcophagus.

We went to Russia and the Scandinavian countries, we climbed on a glacier, shopped in a souk in Morocco, and we took advantage of the hot mud springs in New Zealand, and snorkeled on the Great Barrier Reef. The great cathedrals of Europe were on our itineraries, as were the ruins of Pompei and Mount Olympus.

We walked on the Great Wall of China and visited the terracotta warriors at Xian. Perhaps the most memorable of all, however, was the wet, stormy night we stayed at a little inn on the Bay of Dingle in Ireland. We did so many things together, and we were always together. Now, suddenly, there were no longer two of us.

John and I at the Great Wall of China

His death affected me in ways that I did not anticipate. Regardless of what you do, you are never really prepared for that final separation. At first, the many tasks associated with the passing of a loved one – burial matters, grave markers, insurance policies, legal matters, disposing of his personal items of clothing – occupied much of my time, but the day came when all those matters and responsibilities had been resolved. Prayer had always been a central core in my life for as long as I could remember, and I did more praying now than ever before, and I had to face myself. I felt old and helpless in the face of my aloneness. I was 74 years old. I suppose that I was in deep depression, but I did not choose to talk about this with acquaintances. After all, they had their own lives and their own concerns, and I did not feel that close to any of them. I had never worn my heart on my sleeve, nor was I a person who enjoyed talking about my concerns and problems with others, although I had been the confidante for many of my acquaintances.

Books had always been an escape for me, but now I found that I could not read the way I used to and my life became a rather aimless existence of meaningless routines. I seldom left my home unless it was absolutely necessary. An inner voice kept telling me to get up off my butt and do something – anything but nothing.

I believe that God speaks to each of us in ways we do not always recognize as His voice. Faith is important to the human existence. My mother was a woman of great faith and strength, and she accomplished remarkable things. She lost a husband at a very young age and was left with three children and a mother-in-law to provide a home for, and she did it with remarkable grace. She instilled in me the importance of faith in the future.

We are more than just a spark of energy that flickers out at death. Faith is what gives us strength to face each day with all of its joys and its sorrows. I do not believe that anything happens without a purpose, and although we cannot always see that purpose, there is the assurance that "God's in His heaven and all's right with the world." His ways are mysterious, indeed.

I logged onto the internet one night and began surfing various websites. Somehow, I found myself on the Coastal Pet Rescue website and the little scruffy face that confronted me was that of a little Silky terrier mix the rescuers had christened "Walter." Who on earth would name a dog "Walter"?

Then I began an argument with myself. I did not need a dog. I was too old. Any dog would outlive me. My days of walking a dog several times a day were over. If I contacted the agency, I knew that someone had already adopted this adorable little creature. Like all good, logical, sensible arguments, I lost. I filled out the application papers online, listed Dr. Lester as a reference, clicked "Send," and sat back, wondering what on earth I had done.

For every action there is an equal and opposite reaction. My phone rang a few days later and a voice asked if I was the person who had contacted Coastal Pet Rescue about "Walter." After admitting that I was that person, she told me that her name was Meredith Sutton and asked if she could come by with "Walter" for a visit and I agreed.

"Walter" came into my house and warily examined every nook and corner. He was a little reserved, but then again, he was in a strange place. He was pretty much house-trained and very calm. Meredith and I chatted while he explored, but then suddenly, he jumped into my lap and kissed me.

Meredith had rescued him from the streets when she saw him following some young children on their way to school. They were feeding him Cheetos. She asked who owned him, and a small boy told her, "His name is Busta and he used to be mine. He peed on the rug at home and my mom threw him out and said she did not want him anymore." Thus, Busta, not yet a year old wandered the streets, dirty, flea-ridden and matted, looking for food and affection. The children tried to feed him what junk food they could find. Meredith spoke to the mother, who confirmed the child's story and told her she could have the dog.

After a bath and trip to the vet where he was neutered, micro chipped, and given shots, "Busta," now named "Walter" was ready to be adopted into a forever home. He moved right in with a minimum of fuss, and proceeded to rescue this old lady who didn't know what to do with herself. Although I wasn't sure exactly what I had gotten myself into, one thing was very certain, he was not a "Walter" nor was he a "Busta." I had always been a fan of John Steinbeck and particularly liked his much-disputed story, "Travels with Charley." Raised in a strong Scottish community, I was very familiar with the exploits of Bonnie Prince Charlie. I was also a fan of Charlie Sheen. There are a large number of famous people named Charlie. I think Charlie is a cool name, and so "Walter née Busta" became "Charlie."

Charlie quickly learned his name and has adapted to life with an eccentric old lady. As friends have told me, "Charlie hit the jackpot!" So how has this affected Charlie's life? Well, he is obviously a happy little fellow when you meet him for the first time. He is a people dog and makes friends easily. He makes people smile. When I walk him down Bull Street, he visits with everyone he meets whether he knows them or not. We walk through Chippewa Square – made famous as the place where Forrest Gump sat on the bench – and Charlie has no compunction about jumping up on a bench and visiting with tourists and children. He loves children and babies and adores being petted. Some have called him the Mayor of Chippewa Square because he greets everyone he meets. He walks to Forsyth Park every day, and greets friends, old and new, along the way. He has lately become known as the Mayor of Bull Street as well. Regardless of his titles, he is most definitely a politician. No doubt, many a tourist has returned to their home with a picture of Charlie sitting between them on a park bench, or being hugged by their adoring children. He is most certainly a goodwill ambassador for the city of Savannah.

Charlie has a "BONE" account at Wells Fargo. His only complaint with the bank is that when he walks that way on Bull Street, they are sometimes closed and he can't go in. Living in the home of an avowed reader, he also visits the Homerun Video and Comic book store on Liberty Street. He rushes in when the door is open and runs behind the counter where Chuck gives him a Milkbone. He goes to the dog park several times a week to see his friends Olive, Sarge, Lanie, Kelly, Dobie, Penny, and Pharo. He loves to be chased because he is so fast, and when the dogs start chasing, each other it is pure joy to watch. He splashes in the wading pool with his friends. On our trips to North Carolina, he has two Corgi friends Henry and Stella and they love to chase him too.

So, what has Charlie's coming into my life done for me? Well, if Charlie hit the jackpot, then I have most definitely won the lottery. I have started writing again, which is something I had put on hold when John was sick. My faith in a power that is greater than me has been renewed and I feel stronger. I have become more accepting and less rigid in dealing with others. I am no longer afraid to live, and I am no longer afraid to give my heart to a little 15-pound dog.

Because of Charlie, I have gotten out of the house and have met new people at the dog park and in the neighborhood while walking Charlie. He makes me laugh and enjoy things again. I wake up every morning and find his head on the pillow next to me, and as soon as my eyes open, I am treated to unlimited doggy kisses. It is unconditional love. Because of Charlie, I have to walk and so I get health benefits from him as well. We take long walks in the soft Dixie mornings, we hear the sweet trills of the mockingbirds, and we inhale the sweet scent of magnolias in bloom. We meet people, and talk to people. I am no longer free to do nothing. Slowly, I am healing.

I have found my way once more. It may not be a way for everyone, but it is my way. Charlie makes it all happen, and life is slowly beginning to have meaning again. Yes, I do have those moments when everything seems to close in on me, but I am finding a deep spiritual health that helps me over the rough spots. I will never get over my sense of loss, but I have learned that acceptance comes with time, and Charlie is there to help smooth out the rough spots.

Acknowledgements

The following people contributed much to this book. They provided information, fresh perspectives on certain tales and people. Some of them even appeared in this book.

Bragg, Jane M.
Clary, Polly Connor
Durden, Judy Winkelmes
Ernst, Sgt. Gregory, former Metro Canine Unit of Savannah
Holyoak, Ken
Jenkins, Dorothy C.
Jurgenson, Paul
Locklear, Sanford
Piechocinski, John J.
Ray, William S., Corp., SCMPD
Sanderson, Leslie, R.Ph
Sanford, Norren
Scott, Margaret Ryals
Stiles, John "Jack" R., Jr.
Stubbs, Elsworth
Thompson, Lilla McDougald
Thurlow, Allison
Yongue, Millie

I also wish to thank those dedicated "Yankees" who unwittingly provided fodder for this book.

263

Selected End Notes

The following sources provided much of the information on Litchfield Plantation on page119:

Abstract of Wills, Chatham Co., GA Will Bk. E
Candler, Revolutionary War Records of Georgia, 1:454
GHQ – Vol. LXXX Summer 1996 No. 2
Frank Rossiter SMN 12-15-1968 The Ancient Tomb I-95 Won't Budge
Louisville Gazette 8/1/1801
Col. Mus 7/30/1801 – obit.

Some of the information on the Marietta Cemetery came from the following sources:

Kirby, Joe "Marietta Statue Honors Woman Who Saved Confederate Cemetery." *Civil War News, November 2004.*
Phillips Legion, Co. M. Denmead Volunteers, GA Infantry Battalion
http://www.angelfire.com/ga2/PhillipsLegion/InfCoM.html

For Further Reading

American National Biography, Oxford University Press, New York 1999. Vol. 6, pp. 833-834

Dial, Adolph and Eliades. David K. *The Only Land I Know, A History of the Lumbee Indians.* The Indian Historian Press, San Francisco, 1975.

Evans, W. McKee. *To Die Game: The Story of the Lowry Band, Indian Guerillas of Reconstruction.* Louisiana State University Press. Baton Rouge, 1971.

Sherwood's *Gazetteer*

Golden, Harry. *A Little Girl Is Dead.* The World Publishing Company, New York. 1965.

Jones, C. C., Jr. *The Dead Towns of Georgia.* Reprinted in 1997 by The Oglethorpe Press, Inc., Savannah, Georgia

Savannah River Plantations, edited by Mary Granger. Reprinted in 1997 by Oglethorpe Press, Savannah, Georgia.

Shields, Larry, "The Two Loves of Capt'n Sam." *The Savannah Morning News Magazine*, June 30, 1965.

Stokes, Durwood. *The History of Dillon County, South Carolina.* Univ. of South Carolina Press, Columbia, SC. 1978.

Thomas, Rev. J. A. W., *A History of Marlboro County, with Traditions and Sketches of Numerous Families,* Regional Publishing Company, Baltimore. 1971.

Woodward, C. Vann. *Tom Watson: Agrarian Rebel,* Macmillan Company, New York. 1938.

White, George, Screven *County, Georgia. History & Biographies Taken from Memoirs of Georgia & Historical Collection of Georgia.* Reprint. 2001

www.ingramcontent.com/pod-product-compliance
Lightning Source LLC
Chambersburg PA
CBHW070344090426
42733CB00009B/1276